the series on school reform

Patricia A. Wasley
University of Washington

Ann Lieberman
Senior Scholar, Stanford University

Joseph P. McDonald
New York University

SERIES EDITORS

The Power of Protocols:
An Educator's Guide to Better Practice, 3rd Ed.
JOSEPH P. MCDONALD, NANCY MOHR, ALAN DICHTER,
& ELIZABETH C. MCDONALD

What Should I Do?
Confronting Dilemmas of Teaching in Urban Schools
ANNA ERSHLER RICHERT

Finnish Lessons: What Can the World Learn
from Educational Change in Finland?
PASI SAHLBERG

The Networked Teacher: How New Teachers Build
Social Networks for Professional Support
KIRA J. BAKER-DOYLE

How Teachers Become Leaders:
Learning from Practice and Research
ANN LIEBERMAN & LINDA D. FRIEDRICH

Peer Review and Teacher Leadership:
Linking Professionalism and Accountability
JENNIFER GOLDSTEIN

Improving the Odds: Developing Powerful Teaching
Practice and a Culture of Learning in Urban High Schools
THOMAS DEL PRETE

The Mindful Teacher
ELIZABETH MACDONALD & DENNIS SHIRLEY

Going to Scale with New School Designs:
Reinventing High School
JOSEPH P. MCDONALD, EMILY J. KLEIN, & MEG RIORDAN

Managing to Change: How Schools Can Survive
(and Sometimes Thrive) in Turbulent Times
THOMAS HATCH

Teacher Practice Online: Sharing Wisdom, Opening Doors
DÉSIRÉE H. POINTER MACE

Teaching the Way Children Learn
BEVERLY FALK

Teachers in Professional Communities:
Improving Teaching and Learning
ANN LIEBERMAN & LYNNE MILLER, EDS.

Looking Together at Student Work, 2nd Ed.
TINA BLYTHE, DAVID ALLEN, &
BARBARA SCHIEFFELIN POWELL

Schools-within-Schools:
Possibilities and Pitfalls of High School Reform
VALERIE E. LEE & DOUGLAS D. READY

Seeing Through Teachers' Eyes:
Professional Ideals and Classroom Practices
KAREN HAMMERNESS

Building School-Based Teacher Learning Communities:
Professional Strategies to Improve Student Achievement
MILBREY MCLAUGHLIN & JOAN TALBERT

Mentors in the Making:
Developing New Leaders for New Teachers
BETTY ACHINSTEIN & STEVEN Z. ATHANASES, EDS.

Community in the Making: Lincoln Center Institute, the
Arts, and Teacher Education
MADELEINE FUCHS HOLZER & SCOTT NOPPE-BRANDON, EDS.

Holding Accountability Accountable:
What Ought to Matter in Public Education
KENNETH A. SIROTNIK, ED.

Mobilizing Citizens for Better Schools
ROBERT F. SEXTON

The Comprehensive High School Today
FLOYD M. HAMMACK, ED.

The Teaching Career
JOHN I. GOODLAD & TIMOTHY J. MCMANNON, EDS.

Beating the Odds:
High Schools as Communities of Commitment
JACQUELINE ANCESS

At the Heart of Teaching: A Guide to Reflective Practice
GRACE HALL MCENTEE, JON APPLEBY, JOANNE DOWD,
JAN GRANT, SIMON HOLE, & PEGGY SILVA, WITH
JOSEPH W. CHECK

Teaching Youth Media: A Critical Guide to Literacy, Video
Production, and Social Change
STEVEN GOODMAN

Inside the National Writing Project:
Connecting Network Learning and Classroom Teaching
ANN LIEBERMAN & DIANE WOOD

Standards Reform in High-Poverty Schools:
Managing Conflict and Building Capacity
CAROL A. BARNES

Standards of Mind and Heart:
Creating the Good High School
PEGGY SILVA & ROBERT A. MACKIN

Upstart Startup:
Creating and Sustaining a Public Charter School
JAMES NEHRING

(Continued)

the series on school reform, *continued*

The

POWER

of

PROTOCOLS

An Educator's Guide to Better Practice

THIRD EDITION

Joseph P. McDonald
Nancy Mohr
Alan Dichter
Elizabeth C. McDonald

Teachers College, Columbia University
New York and London

Published by Teachers College Press, 1234 Amsterdam Avenue, New York, NY 10027

Library of Congress Cataloging-in-Publication Data

McDonald, Joseph P.
  The power of protocols : an educator's guide to better practice / Joseph P. McDonald, Nancy Mohr, Alan Dichter, and Elizabeth C. McDonald.—Third Edition.
    pages cm.—(The series on school reform)
    Includes bibliographical references and index.
    ISBN 978-0-8077-5459-7
    1. High schools—United States—Examinations. 2. Educational tests and measurements—United States. 3. Grading and marking (Students)—United States. 4. Teachers—United States—Training of. I. Title.
    LB3060.285.U6M44 2013
    373.1102—dc23   2013018824

ISBN 978-0-8077-5459-7 (paper)

Printed on acid-free paper
Manufactured in the United States of America

20   19   18   17   16   15   14   13   8 7 6 5 4 3 2 1

This third edition of her work and ours
honors the memory of Nancy Mohr

Contents

Preface to the Third Edition

IT HAS BEEN a decade since our coauthor, the late Nancy Mohr, took the photo on the cover. Residents and visitors to New York may recognize the two buildings depicted in this photo. Both are part of the landscape of the Twin Towers attacked on September 11, 2001. The buildings are now just across the street from the Memorial. The one in the background of the photo has the boxy windows that seemed to Nancy an apt image of the kind of work life our book aimed to disrupt—teachers, for example, working largely within cells, separated in time and space from all the colleagues on whom their own success ultimately depends. The cells in this case are viewed from inside the curvilinear building next door. Called the Winter Garden, it is built of glass supported by gracefully arcing steel. One might have considered the Winter Garden for all its glass to be the most vulnerable structure at the foot of its once-giant neighbors. But its steel withstood the attack, and the building became the first structure following 9/11 to be restored and to reopen. Nancy's photo celebrates this reopening. As a book cover, the photo also captures metaphorically the underlying power of protocol: strength in the service of transparency, discovery, and expression. In the protocols we describe in this book, the strength derives (as in all other kinds of protocols) from the constraints they impose. We would say that they constrain participation in order to heighten its effect. Here Nancy's image is also telling: The curvilinear trumps the cellular. The curving steel and all that glass seem not just counterpoint to the stony boxes next door, but provocation.

So it is with protocols too. Their artifice sets them apart from ordinary activity and implicitly raises questions: What if ordinary activity were more like this? What if people stopped to listen to other people's takes on the important educational problems at hand? What if the problems were deliberately unpeeled layer by layer? What if we took time to read student work closely? What if everyone's voice were heard at the meeting, everyone's perspective valued? What if lots of people in every educational organization were as skillful in facilitating genuine conversation as so many now are at avoiding it, suppressing it, or smothering it with self-centered talk?

Ah, you may think, another book about process, when what educators really need is to focus on product. But we think that good product is the outcome of thoughtful process. Indeed, education is first of all process, though it always deals in content and aims to produce worthy outcomes. There is no way, for example, to solve a complex educational problem without listening to the perspectives on the problem of all those affected by it. There is no way to gain the full value of outside expertise without subjecting it to dialogical encounters with internal expertise. And there is no way to engage in productive conflict without expressing it in ways that clarify its dimensions. The protocols we present here help with these and many other processes crucial to educational success in the 21st century: learning from data, analyzing needs, honing theories of action, giving and receiving effective criticism, and making the most of others' ideas.

This third edition of our book has eleven new protocols, a whole new chapter on working for change, and a new one as well on working toward equity. Both previous editions referred to equity as a principle of good facilitation, as it certainly is. But it can be a goal of protocols too. Thus our colleagues around the world who have designed protocols have often done so in the interest of illuminating and confronting inequities in educational institutions, practices, and outcomes. In the new equity chapter, we draw on this work. Also in this third edition, we address more fully than before the role of protocols in teaching. It turns out that educators who use protocols use them today as much in their teaching as they do in their meetings. This is the result of a predictable migration of practice: Educators introduced to protocols at professional meetings quickly surmise their suitability for lesson planning. This migration has so escalated recently that we think it reasonable today to speak of a "protocol pedagogy." This provides an often elusive (from the perspective of more traditional pedagogies) mix of participation, individualization, and structure. The mix is hugely valuable at a time when teachers at all levels are more attuned than before to the diversity of their students' learning backgrounds and skills. It's especially valuable in online teaching, since protocols help ameliorate the sense of isolation that online learners sometimes feel. If you would like to know more about protocol pedagogy and protocols online, check out another book that three of us coauthored (with Janet Mannheimer Zydney) called *Going Online with Protocols: New Tools for Teaching and Learning* (2012). It's a great companion for this book.

Indeed, there are other great companions which we cite throughout the book. In the decade since this book was first published, protocol development and use have become widespread, and protocols themselves very diverse. The best we can do here is to capture some diverse types in sufficient detail, then tell our readers where to find others and, of course, invite them to create still more. Protocol work is, as they say in the online world, an open-source adventure.

The book is organized by categories of use: protocols to work *on practice*, to work *for change*, to work *with texts*, and to work *toward equity*. But we encourage lots of cross-use, lots of improvisation, and lots of adaptation. Other authors with such intentions might say that their book is "not a cookbook." But we think of cookbooks differently, and the difference runs to the heart of what we mean by protocol. Nancy Mohr was a great cook—in fact, this book was conceived while its other authors (and our editor) sat in Alan and Nancy's kitchen as she chopped vegetables. She was also a connoisseur and collector of cookbooks, and especially liked the ones that not only empower the cook with good designs and reliable procedures, but also provide an explicit or implicit invitation to play. She liked, for example, James Haller's (1978) *The Blue Strawberry Cookbook: Cooking (Brilliantly) Without Recipes*. It proclaims—against all tradition—that pesto can be just as well made with any green, nut, and cheese. She also liked Judith Barrett and Norma Wasserman's (1987) *Risotto*, which firmly asserts the tradition of risotto's four distinct "movements"—*soffrito, riso, brodo,* and *condimenti*—but encourages as much variation within them as Beethoven or Mozart managed to obtain within other constraints. Nancy also liked Patricia Wells's (2001) *Paris Cookbook*, with the author's "What I learned" notes on each recipe—as if inviting dialogue between authors and cooks—though she also appreciated the occasional firm guidance in such dialogue, like Wells's advice on page 181: "This is one of those simplest dishes that must be followed to the letter." We have a couple of notes like that in our book too—generally ones that Nancy insisted upon.

Because we encourage improvisation, but also because we know that many facilitators (like cooks) find it helpful to have at hand a quick, at-a-glance guide to the steps of the protocols they facilitate, we have prepared abbreviated versions of all the protocols presented in this book. These are available at the Teachers College Press website (www.teacherscollegepress.com). Readers can download them to their own computers, print them out as needed for their own use (and the use of other protocol participants as they like), and later customize them in any way for future use.

Acknowledgments

THE USE OF protocols in the education of educators has roots in the efforts of at least two generations of scholars and practitioners who have attempted to bring to education insights from the fields of organizational development and human relations training. We think, for example, of the work of two scholar-teachers who provided us important counsel: Don Schön and Matt Miles. A generation of school reformers have made the use of protocols pervasive, many of them influenced by the work of Ted Sizer. We especially acknowledge the indispensable overall contributions of David Allen, Daniel Baron, Fred Bay, Tina Blythe, Victor Cary, Lois Easton, Frances Hensley, Steve Seidel, and Gene Thompson-Grove. We are grateful also to others whose work is reflected in one way or another in the pages of this book. They include Michael Alexander, Elliot Aronson, Patricia Averette, Deb Bambino, Ron Berger, Wendy Brannen, Patricia Carini, Carter Clawson, Simon Clements, Anthony Conelli, Faith Dunne, Peter Elbow, Paula Evans, Helen Featherstone, Howard Gardner, Camilla Greene, Glynda Hull, Steve Jubb, Bena Kallick, Jean King, Jennifer Krumpus, Debbie Laidley, Terra Lynch, John Mauriel, Debbie McIntyre, Robert Miller, Ruth Mitchell, David Niguidula, Vivian Orlen, Rosa Pietanza, Barbara Powell, Stevi Quate, Juli Quinn, Stephanie Robinson, Marlene Roy, Frank SanFelice, Judith Scott, Glenn Singleton, Anna Smith, Gillian Smith, Steven Strull, Pat Wasley, Viv White, Janet Zydney, and the administrators of New York City's Alternative Schools District.

We also acknowledge institutions that have played a generative role in the emergence and popularization of protocols for all the purposes we describe in this book. They especially include the School Reform Initiative, the Coalition of Essential Schools, the Annenberg Institute for School Reform, Harvard Project Zero, the Bay and Paul Foundation, the National Equity Project (formerly known as the Bay Area Coalition for Equitable Schools), NYU's Metro Center and its Metro Learning Communities, CEI-PEA and its PICCS Project, and Teachers College Press.

CHAPTER 1

Basic Practices

W<small>E BEGIN THIS</small> chapter with an overview of four practices that underlie all the protocols that we describe in the following chapters. Then we discuss what research has to say about protocols.

LEARNING THROUGH CONSTRAINTS

Protocols, as we use the term, were first developed by school reformers in the 1990s, based on some earlier prototypes. They share the name and certain features of the protocols long associated with experimental science, computer science, social science, medicine, and diplomacy. For example, they have built-in constraints. The idea is that under the right circumstances constraints are liberating. To demonstrate this benefit, we examine three seminal protocols here. They are seminal because considerable numbers of participants who have experienced them have pronounced the experience worthwhile—the constraints notwithstanding. Thus the protocols have been adapted count-less times in many settings and for diverse purposes. They are popular too because each implicitly teaches one of three rare but important skills: the first, how to give and receive safe and honest feedback; the second, how to analyze complex problems carefully and without rushing to judgment; and the third, how to ground interpretations of complex texts—for example, student work or school data—in close "readings" of the texts.

The first of these protocols is the Tuning Protocol. A full description of it leads off Chapter 3. It was developed by Joe McDonald with colleagues at the Coalition of Essential Schools, and it is among the most constraining of protocols. So the protocol allots a constrained number of minutes to one participant's uninterrupted presentation—say, of a proposal to revamp a cur-riculum. This is followed by a constrained number of minutes for the other participants to *tune* the proposal. They do this by providing uninterrupted feedback in the form of separate *warm* and *cool* comments. The warm ones focus on strengths, and the cool ones on weaknesses. Ensuring what is per-haps the protocol's most significant constraint, the facilitator of a Tuning Protocol insists that the warm and cool feedback stay balanced but separate.

Indeed, he or she may even cut off a reviewer in midsentence if the reviewer starts out warm and then turns cool within the same comment. "Give each your full attention," the facilitator may explain. "Otherwise, the presenter may think the warm is merely sugarcoating for the cool." The protocol ends with a chance for the presenter to reflect on the feedback and to respond to it (again in uninterrupted fashion). Typically, presenters reserve some parts of the feedback for further thought and later response (maybe by email or simply another draft), and the facilitator reminds everyone that the tuning is part of a longer process, not the concluding step (McDonald, Zydney, Dichter, & McDonald, 2012).

The second seminal protocol, called The Consultancy, features an entirely different set of equally rigorous constraints. It too is more fully described in Chapter 3. The Consultancy forces open-minded exploration to start, then speculation. It was developed by Gene Thompson-Grove, Paula Evans, and Faith Dunne in their work at the Coalition of Essential Schools and the Annenberg Institute for School Reform (see www.schoolreforminitiative.org/doc/consultancy.pdf). On one level, its goal is to help participants manage dilemmas in their practice more effectively, but it aims to expand their question-posing skills too—and thus their perceptual capacity. In the process, it also constrains the kinds of questions they can ask. Thus a participant serving as a "presenter" asks a focusing question about a practice-based dilemma that they present to other participants serving as "consultants." Good focusing questions capture succinctly what the presenter hopes to learn from the consultants, and the tensions inherent in the dilemma. They also implicitly signal that the presenter's needs—not the consultants'—should take precedence. For their part, the consultants learn to ask clarifying questions meant to ferret out the elements of what may be for them a novel situation, but without imposing premature interpretive frames or pressing (yet) for deeper analysis. A good clarifying question might inquire about details not covered in the presentation but possibly important nonetheless. By definition, these are easy questions for the presenter to answer because they are factual from his or her perspective. If he or she hesitates to answer, then the facilitator quickly intervenes and rules out the question as not really a clarifying question and likely a probing one instead. Probing questions extend the discipline of the protocol beyond fact gathering into genuine client-centered consulting. They are designed to push the presenter's thinking without imposing the consultant's own interpretation or "solution." Once all clarifying questions are answered (or ruled out), the consultants may move on to probing ones—though only after a gentle warning from the facilitator to avoid any temptation they may feel to solve the presenter's problem or give advice by means of their questions. The facilitator might say that the role of probing questions is to press the presenter to think further and deeper without implying what he or she may find there (Allen & Blythe, 2004; McDonald et al., 2012).

The third seminal protocol is the Collaborative Assessment Conference, developed by Steve Seidel and his colleagues at Harvard Project Zero. It is described more fully in Chapter 5. In this protocol participants describe student work in exclusively low-inference ways at first—a constraint that most newcomers to the protocol experience as a severe one. Thus in response to a typical first question for a Collaborative Assessment Conference, "What do you *see* in this child's drawing?" participants must not say things like "good hand coordination" or even "the stick figure of a child." The facilitator steers them instead to responses like "the color red" and "blue and green lines intersecting just off center on the paper." The point of starting and staying for some time with low-inference seeing is to prepare the group to see the unexpected. Next, the participants respond to the prompt, "What questions does this work raise for you?" Primed by the *seeing*, their *questioning* often goes deep into the work, the student's experience, and the learning context. Finally, they are asked to *speculate* about what a particular student is working on. Here they may discover that the student is not just working on the teacher's assignment, but on an implicit agenda of his or her own construction. All the while, the participant who has brought the work stays quiet—taking in what the others say. At the end, however, the facilitator asks, "Having heard all this, what are your thoughts?" Then the protocol turns into open conversation (McDonald et al., 2012; Seidel, 1998).

Although many protocols are less constraining than these three seminal ones, all feel nonetheless artificial to most novice protocol users—a function of the constraints they impose. "Why can't we just talk?" these novices may say. But their facilitators typically urge them instead to tolerate awhile the discomfort of the constraints. "It's like a game," they may say, echoing Douglas Thomas and John Seely Brown (2011), who write that the boundaries of a game are not just constraints but also potential catalysts for innovation. This is the allure of both games and protocols, and also part of their payoff. Besides, the facilitators might add, "just talking" can lead to talk full of obfuscation and indirection. By contrast, protocols tend to move things along—simply because they often structure in movement. For example, the protocols described above typically conclude with the presenter's reflections on possible next steps toward revising a proposal, resolving a dilemma, or working with a particular student.

Still, in some educational organizations protocols may be received as unwarranted interference in ordinary business. The more dysfunctional this business, the stronger the negative reaction may be. For example, schools or colleges mired in norms of private practice and used to ignoring the actual impact of the practice on students' learning, may not take easily to learning with protocols. Encouraged to try them anyway, however, and pressed to see them all the way through, even reluctant participants may find them refreshing. And urged to reflect on the nature of this refreshment, the participants may then find that the protocols help them imagine alternatives to ordinary habits of working together, learning, and leading.

On the other hand, protocols are not for all occasions, nor should their constraints be allowed to become straitjackets. We have seen some groups so attentive to "doing the protocol" that they lose sight of the purpose. We think that the forms and tones of all meetings for any purpose should always suit the purpose.

EDUCATING OURSELVES

The second basic practice that informs this book is self-education or what we refer to here in the first-person plural (for reasons we discuss below) as "educating ourselves." This is the only means by which professionals generally and educators in particular can direct their education toward the management of their real problems. It is also the only way we educators can direct our education toward meeting the real needs of our students. The main reason is that these problems and needs are vastly more complex than they typically appear to others. Inside perspectives are therefore crucial to understanding them (Lampert, 2001). Indeed, professional development activities for educators that are designed and conducted without benefit of inside perspectives are usually not worth the time and money they cost. Worse, they often involve a kind of de-skilling inasmuch as they discount or dismiss the subtleties of dealing with real complexity. On the other hand, saying that we need to educate ourselves does not mean that we should cut ourselves off from outside sources of learning. On the contrary, we desperately need what outside expertise can offer. It is just that we cannot effectively use it except in combination with our own intimate knowledge of practice.

Our use of the first-person plural in naming and discussing this basic practice acknowledges the fact that the work is necessarily collective. No educator works alone, although we sometimes seem to. Yes, we make lots of private moves, and our work demands an individual capacity for spontaneity, improvisation, and good judgment. But all our efforts, for better or worse, are mediated by the efforts of our colleagues. What they do matters as much to the learning of our students and the running of our programs as what we do. Thus our colleagues' values, standards, and methods are our business—as ours are their business—and the problems of practice are inescapably mutual ones. For this reason, we must give up a pervasive tendency in some educational settings to try to manage these problems alone. Indeed, we may even fail to see what our actual problems of practice are unless we dare to inquire about them together. This is because so much of our knowledge of practice is tacit and becomes subject to critique only when we reflect on it in the company of others (Schön, 1983).

Of course, protocol-based conversations are hardly our only means of learning from each other. John Seeley Brown and others studying work life inside the Xerox Corporation in the 1980s and early 1990s found that informal conversations can be hugely valuable. They documented the learning power and productivity boost of work-focused but off-task conversations among repair mechanics hanging out together—literally at the water cooler among other places (Brown & Duguid, 2000; Brown & Gray; 1995; Wenger, 1998). One of us studying the efforts to replicate a small high school found the same advantage among teachers having some beers together at a bar on a late Friday afternoon (McDonald, Klein, & Riordan, 2009). Meanwhile, formal conversations that are not protocol-based are also valuable. We merely warn against the kind that involve what Emily White (2006) calls "under-regulated talking." Everyone knows this kind—where the leader talks too much, and lets others talk too much too. Together these talkers choke off real listening, as well as the kind of distributed and beyond-one's-comfort-zone learning that is often needed in conversations about education.

In this book, we advocate a mix of formal methods and informal methods for educators educating ourselves and for working together in other ways. And among the formal methods, we advocate a limited but strategic use of formal protocols, as well as a liberal use of informal adaptations of them. "Okay," a facilitator might say without using the P-word, "let's see if we can get a little more clarity on what we all think by doing a quick go-round. And to make it more fun, let's avoid repeating what any previous speaker in the round has said in the hope of turning up fresh perspectives." See the All-Purpose Go-Round protocol in Chapter 2.

LEARNING FROM CLOSE TEXTUAL ANALYSIS

One of the seminal protocols we described above, namely, the Collaborative Assessment Conference, requires educators to pause periodically in their practice and become deliberate students of their students. The point is to reach a different understanding of students than we may be used to, one deeper than what is required merely to keep our teaching and their learning in sync. This involves close textual analysis—the third practice that underlies this book—and it demands a great shift of energy. Instead of pressing for student work flow as educators usually do, judging quickly the value of the flow's direction, we suspend flow, capture images of the work interrupted, study the images calmly and deliberately, and explore together what they may mean. Along with a broad alliance of teachers, school leaders, teacher educators, and reform-minded educators with many other job titles, we often refer to this great shift of energy with the simple phrase "looking at student work" (Allen, 1998; Blythe, Allen, & Powell, 1999/2007). Here, however, we acknowledge that the looking we advocate is simple in the deep and disciplined way that Thoreau's looking was simple at Walden Pond and Annie Dillard's at Tinker Creek: simple but elemental, simple but difficult.

We read students' work closely and collectively for two reasons. One is to learn more about the students' learning—to gain clues about their strengths and weaknesses, their misconceptions, their proximity or distance from a conceptual breakthrough, their progress with respect to some defined standard, or their unique ways of thinking and working. And we read their work closely to appraise the efficacy of our own work. Their text is thus our text. It is where our moves as educators and their impact on our students are most traceable (McDonald, 2001, 2002). It is where the strengths and weaknesses of our practice—individual and collective—become most apparent. For this reason, our efforts to explore student work *together* are crucial to our efforts to revise and improve the collective work of our educational institutions. They are at the heart of educational change.

One of the challenges of looking together at student work derives from an occupational hazard—namely, that our own belief in the efficacy of our efforts as educators is a principal tool of our trade. Even when our students seem resistant, it is partly our persistence in believing in the possibilities of their learning that gives them in time the faith they need to perform well. We learn early on the job that we must project confidence in the directions we offer our students, or they lose faith in these directions. However, our unconditional believing can hurt our capacity to revise our practice when needed. It may also encourage us to hide the real complexities of our work from our students, and inadvertently even from ourselves. That is, we may project such confidence in the directions we set that we conceal the choices, hunches, inescapable uncertainty, and arbitrariness that underlie them. Over time, this habit may insulate us from the gaps and faults of our own expertise, and seal us off from new expertise. Dangerously, for both our students and us, it can also mask the real dynamics of learning.

Meanwhile, as we show in Chapter 4, protocols for working toward educational change include many that focus on other kinds of texts besides student work. By *texts*, we mean renderings of thought and experience in any medium (Scholes, 1985). Historically, much of the appeal of protocols like the Tuning Protocol and the Consultancy has been that they press educators to render dimensions of their practice into texts for study. These, of course, include student work that has resulted from the practice, but they also include transcriptions of observations, journals, videotapes of educational life, teaching plans, and composed accounts of dilemmas and problems. Text-based protocols of various kinds prompt practitioners to create such texts and thus pause from practice, extract some experience from it worth examining for whatever reason, then shift energy from "doing" practice to "reading" it (McDonald, 1992; Schön, 1983). This reading is best undertaken in trustworthy collegial groups. Now, of course, with handheld sound and video recorders as close as one's cellphone, the task of rendering practice into text is far easier than it once was and, perhaps as a result, less revelatory in itself. Still, the collective reading of a text by others remains hugely valuable—to the text writers *and* readers.

Many text-based protocols follow what is called a "semiotic approach." *Semiotics* is the practice of textual analysis common in literary, media, and cultural studies (Eagleton, 1983; Scholes, 1985). It involves analyzing both the surfaces and deeper features of the texts. As we suggest in *Going Online with Protocols*, text-based protocols are very useful for learning from and among what is the largest collection of texts ever assembled in human history—namely, the World Wide Web (McDonald et al., 2012).

PRACTICING TRANSPARENCY

The fourth basic practice underlying the book is what we call "transparency." It is premised on the idea that educators gain cognitive and ethical leverage when they make the effort to reveal their teaching intentions (increasingly commonplace today as a result of the focus on learning standards), and also when they take the time to illuminate the learning challenges for students in responding to these intentions. Protocols tend to force this kind of transparency by segmenting elements of a conversation whose boundaries might otherwise blur—particularly for the least verbally adept students—for example, the boundaries between describing and judging, or supporting and critiquing. By artificially segmenting these things, protocols afford unusual opportunities for students to learn the differences if they do not already know them, or to practice fine points if they do. Meanwhile, protocols not only force all students to participate—for example, by structuring in turn-taking—but also force students to listen to each other—for example, by forbidding any repetition in the turn-taking. No one gets to lurk in a protocol, and no one is shut out.

In their transparency, protocols teach us habits that we wish we already had: to take the time to listen and notice, to take the time to think about what we want to say, to work without rushing, to speak less (or speak up more), to give and receive graciously both forthright praise and forthright critique. They can also usefully disturb privacy and certainty by interrupting the ordinary flow of conversation. Some of them force the raising of questions, the suspension of judgment, and the withholding of response—all of these useful to learning at certain times. In their transparency, protocols may also encourage an environment for learning that presumes the social construction of knowledge. For example, protocols like the seminal ones we discussed above are explicitly designed to point out that no one participant all by himself or herself is smart enough to "tune" the proposal, unpack the problem, or elucidate the piece of student work. It takes collaboration—a social act of understanding. Helping learners trust in the social construction of knowledge is a strategy well supported by research on learning that finds that encounters with other people's understanding enable learners to gain and deepen their own (Donovan, Bransford, & Pellegrino, 2000; National Research Council, 2000). Along with John Dewey, we believe that such learning environments can also foster democracy. This is because they implicitly encourage learners—whether they are first graders, graduate students, or colleagues in professional education—to appreciate the value of diverse ideas and deliberative communities (Glickman, 1998; Greene, 1988; Oakes & Lipton, 1999).

WHAT THE RESEARCH SAYS

The consequence of taking seriously the four basic practices—that is, of making room for them in the larger practice of education—is the emergence of a different kind of workplace for teachers and their students. This is one where the power to assess outcomes and to take action to improve them is distributed throughout the organization, and where the people who do the work (teachers and students) are able, willing, and even eager—in consultation with others—to make changes as needed in order to improve the work. Key elements of such settings include the use of teams, both "front-line" (to do the work) and "off-line" (to study ways to improve the work); richer information systems with broader access to them; and the cultivation of a commitment to the organization's mission at all levels, purchased by the decentralization of management authority, accountability, and trust. Management theorists call this a "high-performance workplace" (Applebaum, Bailey, Berg, & Kalleberg, 2000; Fishman, 1996; Ichniowski, Levine, Olson, & Strauss, 2000). And for some time, education researchers have been studying the relevance of its characteristics to the success of educational institutions, particularly schools. In what follows, we review this research. We acknowledge in advance that we find it promising with respect to what we advocate in this book, though with some reservations that we note below.

Based on extensive research across many different contexts, Stanford researchers Milbrey McLaughlin and Joan Talbert (2001, 2006), as well as Talbert alone (2011), describe high-performance schools that consistently engage diverse students in challenging academic work, and keep them engaged and successful over time. A key factor in their success is the presence of what the researchers call "professional communities of practice." These are within-school groups that meet frequently (often using protocols) to examine student work and other data-laden texts together, to think through problems of practice, and to hone their mutual commitment to the learning goals of the school. Fred Newmann and Gary Wehlage (1995), reporting earlier on a national study of 24 "restructured schools," conclude that the most successful "were the ones that used restructuring tools to help them function as professional communities of practice" (p. 3). Where such communities also had the right cultural and structural conditions to exert continual leadership, and where they focused on improving the intellectual quality of their students' work, the work did improve (Newmann & Associates, 1996).

Studies of the impact of what other researchers have called "teacher learning communities" or "teacher teams," and what many practitioners call "critical friends groups" or "professional learning communities," have consistently shown benefits for students, though only when the communities focus explicitly on increasing student learning (Curry, 2008; Little, Gearhart, Curry, & Kafka, 2003; McLaughlin & Talbert, 2006; Phillips, 2003; Supovitz, 2002; Supovitz & Christman, 2003; Vescio, Ross, & Adams, 2008). By contrast, when not focused on student learning, such groups and, yes, the protocols they sometimes employ may have only a superficial impact, even if the participants pronounce them valuable. This was true of many of the small teacher communities that Jon Supovitz and Jolley Christman (2003) studied in Philadelphia and Cincinnati. On the other hand, the Cincinnati teams that used an instructionally focused protocol called Standards in Practice (see Chapter 4 for a description) outperformed teams that did not use the protocol, and also teachers who did use it but not as members of teams (Holtzapple, 2001). Judith Warren Little and her colleagues report similar findings in their study of schools using the Tuning Protocol (see Chapter 3) and the Collaborative Assessment Conference (see Chapter 5). "The value of looking at student work," they conclude, "resides in its potential for bringing students more consistently and explicitly into deliberations among teachers" (p. 192). To the extent that the protocol facilitates this, it is beneficial; otherwise, it is not. They also note that conversations about student work were more productive when groups were flexible in their use of protocols—when, for example, they adjusted time limitations to suit the conversation, or even violated protocol constraints in order to pursue questions of interest (Little et al., 2003; McDonald et al., 2012).

Karen Seashore Louis and her colleagues (Louis, Kruse, & Marks, 1996) argue also that a crucial component of an effective professional community of practice is a focus on student learning, but they acknowledge the importance of other components too: deprivatization of practice, collaboration, shared norms and values, and reflective dialogue. Their list seems a lot like the list of topics we cover in this book, and, of course, each element on the list is harder to implement than it sounds. Moreover, the elements are highly interactive. The first two, for example, require difficult shifts in organizational values and structures. Too many educational organizations today are still focused more on their own smooth running than on student learning, and this smooth running depends in large measure on keeping practice private and serious talk about practice minimal. Some reformers aim to improve matters quickly by pressing directly for a focus on student learning and/or the deprivatization of practice, while paying insufficient attention to the rest of the items on the researchers' list. Similarly, reformers may insist on accountability with respect to certain indicators of student learning such as test scores, but neglect the problem of how educators, used to working alone and ignoring such indicators, might suddenly reverse emphasis. Or they may insist on educators working in teams, but provide no models for how the teams should operate, and no coaching. Or they may provide time for educators to meet together for planning, but no norms for planning or frameworks of values to guide it. Finally, they may train teachers to use protocols but provide them few incentives to try them in a genuine way—for example, in the context of distributed leadership.

In the end, we think it is the workplace itself that matters most—not the individual characteristics that comprise it but the culture these characteristics help generate and sustain. And our promotion of protocols in this book should be read in that light. Indeed, Anthony Bryk and his colleagues at the Chicago Consortium on School Research (Bryk, Sebring, Allensworth, Luppescu, & Easton, 2010) have recently contributed much empirical backing for this theory that the real leverage for school improvement is at the level of the whole institution. Reporting on a large, longitudinal, and painstaking study of Chicago elementary schools, they report that the best performing schools among their sample had high levels of what the researchers call "essential supports": coordinated instruction, a student-centered learning climate, a cohesive professional community, trusting parents and other community stakeholders, and strong leadership. The latter, in the researchers' account, is not just the kind of leadership that keeps things running smoothly, nor even the kind that offers continual instructional guidance too, but also the kind that has been suffused throughout the school in the form of what the researchers call "facilitative leadership." Moreover, the professional community that was found to be characteristic of these high-performing schools is not cohesive because it has been ordered to be, or because it was somehow hired to be, but rather because it works continually on the problem of staying cohesive despite all the temptations to stray.

What we called above the reservations evident in the still emerging research on professional learning communities and protocols are ones that we are very comfortable pointing out. They remind us that these things are after all just tools, and while they can in the right hands and contexts make valuable contributions, they are not panaceas for the problems of educational practice. Nothing we have to say in this book about protocols should be construed as more praise than this. Yet this is hardly faint praise. It is instead as good as it ever gets.

CHAPTER 2

Facilitating

AT ITS HEART, facilitating is about promoting participation, ensuring equity, and building trust. This is true whether the facilitating involves a protocol or another kind of meeting format. The difference is that protocols are deliberately designed with these tasks in mind, while most other meeting formats are rife with opportunities for ignoring them. We all know the result: the faculty meeting that turns into a monologue by the principal or the chairperson, the whole-group discussion that two or three people dominate, or the brainstorming that manages to suppress divergent thinking.

Of course, protocols are no panacea for these or any other kinds of collegial problems, but they are valuable in highlighting the fact that problems frequently surface. In offering colleagues the image of an alternative reality, they may also encourage efforts to address the problems more consistently. Thus someone might say, "Let's have more of the kind of faculty meetings we had that one time, when everyone got a chance to talk, and everybody's ideas got heard and responded to."

To promote participation, ensure equity, and build trust, the facilitator first needs an "appointment." It may be a formal one, as in the announcement that "George will lead the task force"; or it may be informal, as in a colleague asking, "Hey, George, why don't you facilitate the group this time?" In either case, George has to have a full understanding of what the appointment entails. He has to understand that the three tasks—involving participation, equity, and trust—are at the heart of the work he is being asked to do. Furthermore, he must be willing and able to perform the tasks. One aim of this book is to help spread such understanding, willingness, and ability throughout educational organizations. This is crucial, we think, to the effort to make them high-performance workplaces for teachers and students.

SIGNIFICANCE OF THE FACILITATOR'S CORE TASKS

One reason why competent facilitators are in short supply today is that many organizational environments discount the importance of the facilitator's core tasks. The facilitator deals merely with process, some like to say, but what really matters is content: "getting the information across," "accomplishing the task," "making the decision." We believe, however, that content has a way of evaporating in the absence of participation, equity, and trust.

For this reason, we begin our practical advice about facilitating by offering some arguments about why encouraging participation, ensuring equity, and building trust matter so much—and how they relate to content. With such arguments to rely on, the facilitator need not fear the old accusation that he or she is being "touchy-feely."

Promoting Participation

Learning is social. We inevitably learn through and with others, even though what is finally understood is our own mental construction (National Research Council, 2000). In insisting that educators learning together get to know one another first, the facilitator is not just encouraging cordiality. Openness to others' experiences builds openness to others' perspectives, and such openness provides learning opportunities otherwise unavailable.

When the facilitator encourages participants in a protocol to "hear all voices," it is really a call to highlight a sufficient number of perspectives on the issue or problem at hand such that everyone can gain the possibility of new insight. It is also a call to pool knowledge and thus become smarter in the aggregate, to cultivate and rely upon what Lauren Resnick (1987) calls "shared cognition," which she properly distinguishes as the hallmark of most complex work situations outside education. Finally, it is a call to suspend what our friend Paul Naso calls the "ordinary political cross-currents" of schools and colleges—the ones that may cause the newer people to hold their tongues while the veterans speak, that may give some people used to exerting influence more than their due share of it, and that may perpetuate old culture within new structures.

Ensuring Equity

The presumption of a genuinely accountable educational organization is that everyone can learn what one needs to learn in order to do the work at hand. This *everyone* involves adults as well as students. The difficulty in living up to such a presumption comes from the fact that people learn in different ways, including ways that may seem aberrant: the child who persists in walking around or talking out of turn; the adult who seems always to disagree or to digress.

In striving for the inclusion of such people, the facilitator does more than protect their opportunities for learning or smooth out social ripples. He or she also implicitly acknowledges the value of difference in the group's learning, and helps the group strive to understand the contribution that difference may make. In doing so, the facilitator may stretch colleagues' capacity for learning from it. A norm that respects difference is crucial to genuine accountability. Until a professional community really knows and understands the range of viewpoints it contains—however variable and contradictory—it remains incapable of taking collective and effective action on behalf of all its students' learning. That is because it ends up screening out—for the sake of its own false consensus—one or more viewpoints that make up the "collective."

Of course, a facilitator's pursuit of equity must make room not only for difference of viewpoint, but also difference in life experience—derived, for example, from race, ethnicity, class background, sexual orientation, ability/ disability, age, and so on. In many educational settings, however, working on equity in this regard can invite volatile reactions, and require that predictable achievement and opportunity gaps related to race in particular be surfaced and confronted. Those involved in such work know all too well how powerful, emotional, and transformative this work can be for both educators and students who seriously engage in it. Some of the earliest uses of the protocols we discuss in this book were to help communities begin to engage with the equity challenges they were facing. Some protocols were designed specifically to provide a way to enter equity-focused conversations in a safe, facilitated, but substantial way. See, for example, the Paseo in Chapter 6. Other protocols were adapted to ensure that an equity perspective is prominent even if equity is not by itself the only focus. See, for example, the protocol also in Chapter 6, called Looking at Student Work (with Equity in Mind). We like to say that protocols help us develop the habits we wish we had, and that is nowhere more true than in the matter of making room for the equitable expression of diversity. Whether in the pursuit of this crucial dimension of equity or in a confrontation with inequity, protocols can help.

Building Trust

Educators educating themselves rely on one another's honesty, insight, and experience. Going public with their work, they let one another in on what they are doing, thinking, learning, and hoping. They invite one another's perspectives in the expectation that these will be valuable. They invite the collective experience of the group to serve as the arbiter of their own growth. All of these efforts require a trustful situation.

It is important to consider, however, what a trustful situation really is and what it is for. It is situational. When a facilitator promotes a group's trust, it is not to help everyone trust every other individual member as an individual, but rather to help each trust the situation that has been collectively created. The purpose is not trust in general, but trust sufficient to do the work at hand.

Nor is the goal to make everyone feel comfortable. Given trust, a group of individuals can learn from one another and their work together even when the work creates discomfort—as work involving worthwhile learning often does.

THE FACILITATOR'S MOVES

Facilitating protocols involves macroplanning—as in what protocol to use when, and how to open and close the meeting—and also microplanning done in the moment—as in how to intervene when something goes wrong, and when to change one's macroplan. In what follows, we offer some advice about some of the better moves to use at these and other points, and how to use them.

Opening

Sometimes facilitators who use protocols think the people they work with won't need any warm-up. "Well," they say, "I think I'll just start with looking at students' work [or dealing with controversial topics, or planning collaboratively] and skip all of that touchy-feely stuff." In the process, as we suggest above, they may undercut their purpose. Preparing educators to give and get sensitive feedback is not a lightweight distraction or lure. It is the developmentally crucial start of building a professional learning environment. No one can give and get feedback sensitively, honestly, and effectively without first knowing a little bit about everybody else involved, discussing the context in which they are gathered—or what is often called the "agenda"—and setting or reviewing some group norms.

Sometimes facilitators who understand the value of opening moves are nonetheless tempted to skip them because they think there is not enough time. Time is always an issue in the facilitation of groups. In our experience, however, a little investment of time up front saves a lot of time later. What matters most in the selection of an opening move is that the one selected be relevant to the business at hand. Disconnected openers provoke the touchy-feely accusation, and seem as incongruous as an off-color joke at the start of a serious speech. It matters, too, that the scale of the opening move fit the scale of the meeting: short moves for short time frames; longer ones for half-day sessions or daylong retreats. Yet, in either short or long form, the opening moves that should never be skipped are *participant introductions*, *context review* (in particular, the design of the protocol to be used), and *norm-setting*. We explore each of these in turn below.

Participant introductions have two general purposes. The first is to get everybody present to say something right away—something that connects each to the business of the group. People who speak early at a meeting are more likely to avoid the prolonged silence that might otherwise envelop them and become a source of tension for them as well as others. The second purpose is to help everyone know something relevant about each of the people present, and thus represent in a symbolic way the presence of a distributed intelligence. *Context review* includes what the group plans to work on and why, perhaps how it formed, and certainly what it hopes to achieve. It also includes the ways in which the group will work. A protocol usually defines only the last of these; while the others need to be explained, discussed, perhaps negotiated. Meanwhile, one important part of the context—namely, the design of the protocol itself—needs review. Marlene Roy and Terra Lynch who often direct the Facilitative Leadership Workshops for NYU's Metro Learning Communities accomplish the latter by means of the first two steps of what they call "IRDU." An acronym, rather than the misspelling of the national language of Pakistan, IRDU stands for (1) Introduce the protocol with some reference to its history (if known) and its purpose; (2) allow participants to Read through it (no matter how long that takes), and this of course requires having a print-out of its steps (note that steps of all protocols described in this book can be downloaded at the Teachers College Press website); (3) then—and only then—actually Do the protocol; (4) and, finally, explore other Uses for it (more about this step below). *Norm-setting* does not refer to the constraints or steps built into the protocol, but rather to larger behavioral guidelines for being together and learning from one another. For example, norms involve such matters as how participants treat one another's ideas and how they push each other's thinking. They may also involve whether they may talk about what has transpired within the meeting when outside the meeting, and whether they turn off cellphones during the meeting. Norms may even call upon participants to view discomfort not as an avoidable aberration, but as a necessary part of the learning process.

Intervening and Closing

Even though protocols help prevent things from going wrong (by providing an overarching structure that participants can trust), unexpected things still happen that require intervention. Once Joe McDonald was facilitating a protocol in a room where two or three nonparticipants were at the periphery working at computers. Speaking within the parameters of the protocol, one participant began to speak about race, whereupon someone at the periphery interrupted. Joe explained to the person that the group was using a constrained form of conversation, and that if she wanted to join the conversation, she would have to sit at the table and follow the protocol, too. She declined to get involved. Later, however, she interrupted again. At that point, Joe ought to have asked her to leave the room—or, alternatively, moved the protocol to a more private space. Instead, Joe permitted the person to enter the conversation on her own terms, and effectively gave up facilitating the protocol. Later, the participant whose contribution had been interrupted told Joe that he had felt deserted by the one person he had expected to keep the difficult conversation safe. It was clearly a bad move on Joe's part.

Situations demanding facilitator interventions are usually somewhat easier to handle than this. For example, a participant new to the protocol format might momentarily lose the suspension of disbelief that new participants usually need and might say something like: "This is silly. Why don't we just talk?" Generally, a confident admonition to trust the process a little longer, combined with a reminder that the group will debrief the process in the end, is enough to quell the uprising.

Some protocols—for example, variations of the Tuning Protocol— encourage the facilitator to help regulate the conversation by participating in it substantively—for example, offering a supportive (warm) comment to the presenter to offset a string of critical (cool) ones, or pressing for more attention to criteria for reviewing student work. Other protocols, however, discourage this kind of substantive involvement by the facilitator. In such cases, problems that really need intervention require either brief interruptions or longer time-outs. During a time-out, it is useful to engage in some silent activity to help participants gather their thoughts about whatever has provoked the intervention before asking them to discuss it. Merely taking a 10-minute break can also be a useful intervention.

Intervening moves try to preserve or revise the learning process, while closing moves try to ensure that the learning itself carries over into the educators' ordinary work life. The latter is best achieved through metacognition. That is, participants must take the trouble to specify what they have learned—substantively and procedurally—and then to generalize from it. One way the facilitator can help with this transfer is to press participants to answer three questions, ones that are useful to nearly any kind of debriefing:

- *What?* What have I learned about the topic that brought this group together?
- *So what?* What difference does it seem to make to my teaching, for example, or my team's planning?
- *Now what?* What steps can I take to make the most of what I have learned?

These questions require some time for private consideration and for public discussion. Indeed, they constitute a protocol in themselves—one well worth using in a longer meeting such as a daylong retreat. (See schoolreforminitiative. org/doc/what_so_what.pdf. Also see our variation, What Do We Know? What Do We Suspect? What Do We Need to Find Out? in Chapter 4.) When it comes to closing a short meeting, however, short moves work best. And an excellent one is the one that Marlene Roy and Terra Lynch advocate—the last stop of their IRDU design: Now that we've done this protocol (or these protocols) here in this workshop, how do you imagine using it (them) in some other context?

BRIEF PROTOCOLS

Sometimes it is best to open or close a protocol-based meeting with the use of another, briefer protocol—or even to intervene with a briefer protocol-within-a-protocol. This is especially true when time is less of an issue—for example, at a full-morning meeting. In what follows, we describe some brief protocols that can be used as opening, closing, or intervening moves. Then afterward we describe four elaborate protocols that can serve as opening moves for meetings where time is plentiful and a good start crucial—for example, a daylong or multiday retreat.

Postcards

The facilitator says, "Without looking at it first, deal yourself one of the picture postcards from this pack going around. Then imagine why it's the perfect picture for you at this moment [or how it represents your work, or describes your feelings about starting or ending the workshop]. Be prepared to show and tell."

We especially like to use black-and-white "art" cards, because they lend themselves to interpretation. A variation is to have people find the person with the same card (provided there are duplicates available) and discuss their different reactions. Given a smaller supply of postcards, the facilitator might ask two or three people to share the same card. We have also asked participants in a meeting to use their laptops or smart phones to access some trove of online images, and to find one that speaks to them at that moment relative to the meeting getting started (McDonald et al., 2012).

The activity ends with a Go-Round (see the next protocol), in which everybody has a minute to share.

All-Purpose Go-Round

This is perhaps the single most important protocol a facilitator can know. The prompt can be as simple as "Introduce yourself and tell us one thing you like about technology and one thing you dislike." The facilitator should keep it simple by making sure that people don't jump in and that the time frame stays inviolate. One way to do this is to specify a time allotment—say,

30 seconds each—and to signal by using body language when the time is up: intent listening with smiling and nodding, then a nod of the head or shift of the eyes to indicate that it is the next person's turn. Turns can thus be signaled with no facilitator talking at all. See, for example, the protocol in Chapter 4 called What Comes Up?

Clearing

This protocol is also known as Connections. People come to meetings or leave them with things on their minds, and they need time to transition from there to here or here to there. It helps enormously to take the time, from 5 to 10 minutes, for the group members to say what things are on their minds. There are simple rules: Nothing is too irrelevant; there can be no dialogue; each person talks only once unless everyone else has spoken; and silence is okay. When time is up, the facilitator moves on. Facilitators who call this protocol Connections rather than Clearing may suggest that each speaker try to bring what may otherwise seem a disconcerting past bit of business into the present, rather than simply set it aside by acknowledging it. In practice, however, these mental moves are the same. This is an especially good starter for an after-school workshop when people come in still connected to some earlier events, or for a closing when a protocol session has been particularly intense.

Pair-Share

Participants all share with a partner some past experience related to the goals of the meeting. Experiences might include a positive one they have had in a professional workshop, or best and worst experiences taking a test, or an earliest memory of being a student, or something about their first day as a professor. All pairs address the same question, then discuss as a group what their sharing had in common and what surprised them. Obviously, Pair-Share can also provide a useful intervention at times, and a good reflective close, and it need not always involve a reflection on past experience. For example, a group engaged in discussing a complex idea might use Pair-Share to explore their respective understandings of the idea at that moment.

Reflection on a Word

This is an activity associated with Patricia Carini's Prospect Center and its work in Descriptive Review of the Child (Himley, 2000). Before beginning a Review, participants are often asked to focus on a word that the facilitator has chosen with the child in mind. In describing this use, Elaine Avidon (2000) beautifully suggests its power:

We spoke of *enough* as a word of measure having to do with both persons and things, quantity and quality. We placed our depictions of *enough* on a continuum with notions of adequate and appropriate at its center, and too much and too little at the edges. On this continuum, *enough* was a boundary line, a standard either achieved, not yet realized, or exceeded. At issue was whose measure, whose standards, whose evaluation. (p. 36, emphasis in original)

In our adaptation of the protocol, participants introduce themselves briefly, then give their own takes on the word *literacy* (or whatever word seems relevant to the work at hand). This helps everyone see the multiple takes that a word can invoke, and establishes the norm that different takes are useful and helpful to the group's learning overall. This activity can also be a good intervention; taking a moment to clarify—or problematize—a word or term can help clear the air, or generate new insight when it may be especially needed.

LONGER OPENERS

The following long opening moves are described in the same format used to present the rest of the book's protocols. The format begins by introducing the protocol, usually with a reference to its source. Next it acknowledges the particular purpose for which the protocol seems designed. Then it notes important details such as time frame and any materials or special settings required. Next it lays out the steps of the protocol, if it is a multistep one. Whenever we believe that including a time frame for a step will help users, we include one, but mostly we leave the matter up to the facilitator's discretion. Finally—again, in most cases—the format includes some facilitation tips and some possibilities for variation.

Fears and Hopes

We have seen versions of this protocol used to open many kinds of meetings in many different places, including online. Its effectiveness depends on the fact that people rarely undertake a new learning experience without harboring some (usually unexpressed) fears and hopes about what will happen. This protocol gets these into the open.

Some facilitators hesitate to open with a "negative" question such as "What are your fears about this meeting?" Their own fear is that the negativity will get out of hand. However, our experience is quite the opposite. When participants are encouraged to say aloud that they fear the meeting will be boring, will not meet their real needs, or will be run in a way that is insulting to their learning, then they become, paradoxically, much more open and receptive to the work of the actual meeting. Moreover, having accepted this first risk—to speak of their fears aloud—they feel less defensive about other risks that may come their way—including to speak openly of their hopes.

Purpose

One purpose is simply to help people learn some things about one another. But the deeper purpose is to establish a norm of ownership by the group of every individual's expectations and concerns—to get these into the open and to begin addressing them together.

Details

Time for this protocol can vary from 5 to 25 minutes, depending on the size of the group and the range of their concerns. If the group is particularly large, the facilitator asks table groups to work together and then report out. The only supplies needed are individual writing materials, newsprint, markers—or a laptop and projector.

Steps

1. *Introduction.* The facilitator asks participants to write down briefly for themselves their greatest fear for this meeting/workshop/retreat/year/course: "If it proves to be the worst experience you've had, what will have happened here (or not happened)?" Then they write their greatest hope: "If this proves to be one of the best meetings you've ever attended, what will have happened here?"
2. *Pair-Share.* If time permits, the facilitator asks participants to share their hopes and fears with a partner.
3. *Listing.* Participants call out fears and hopes as the facilitator lists them on separate pieces of newsprint or projects them on a screen or whiteboard.
4. *Debriefing.* The facilitator prompts, "Did you notice anything surprising or otherwise interesting while doing this activity? What was the impact on you or others of expressing negative thoughts? Would you use this activity in your school? In your classroom? Why? Why not?"

Facilitation Tips

The facilitator should list all fears and hopes exactly as expressed, without edits, comments, or judgments. One should not be afraid of the worst fears. A meeting always goes better once these are expressed. The facilitator can also participate by listing his or her own fears and hopes. After the list of fears and hopes is complete, the group should be encouraged to ponder them. If some things seem to need modification, the facilitator should say so in the interest of transparency, and make the modifications. If some of the hopes seem to require a common effort to realize, or if some of the fears require a special effort to avoid, the facilitator should say what he or she thinks these are, and solicit ideas for generating such efforts. It is easy to move from here into norm-setting: "In order to reach our hoped-for outcomes while making sure we deal with our fears, what norms will we need?"

Variations

One variation that cuts down on time is to use pictures or picture postcards (or in online environments, downloaded images) that have fairly ambiguous meanings and ask participants to introduce themselves and tell how the images they have picked or been assigned express their hopes or fears for the meeting/course/and so on. In this variation, the facilitator listens carefully and makes notes while participants speak, so as to be able to capture expressed hopes and fears for the group's reflection.

When a group includes distinct subgroups—for example, with respect to work roles or experience with protocols—it is often useful to have a subgroup-share rather than a pair-share in Step 2.

Protocol for Setting Norms

Sometimes facilitators follow Fears and Hopes with this protocol, saying something like, "What norms do we need in order to increase the likelihood that our hopes will be realized and our fears allayed?" Nancy Mohr learned this protocol from Fran Vandiver, a former Florida principal. They were together in a school coaches' training that wasn't going well. Fran suggested that the group set norms, and Nancy thought at first that this was a terrible idea. "After all," she said to herself, "everyone here is an adult." This is a common naive assumption, akin to "Why can't we start off with a long lecture? After all, everyone chose to learn about this topic," or "Why can't we just have a conversation about this controversy or conflict? I'm sure everyone will have something constructive to say."

Purpose

We set norms first of all to curtail some unproductive behaviors (e.g., "Monitor your personal airtime"). We also set them to give ourselves permission to be bolder than we might otherwise be (e.g., "Take some risks here"). And we set them in order to remind ourselves that people learn in different ways (e.g., "Give everybody time to think"). Norms are especially useful when newcomers are likely to arrive after the work is already under way (and this happens frequently in professional learning groups). When newcomers arrive, the norms fill them in (hence the importance of public posting). They don't have to learn them through trial and error. Norms are also useful when "tricky" conversations are likely (and tricky conversations are frequent in real-life groups).

Details

Norm-setting can take 10 minutes or much longer. Once a group that Nancy Mohr was facilitating took an hour to decide whether airtime should be restricted. The vociferous objections to this proposed norm came from a group of men used to dominating meetings they attend. But the norm was set despite their objections, and later one of them confessed publicly how much he had learned from listening for a change. On the other hand, we have seen groups get bogged down in elaborate conversations about norms, often involving "wordsmithing." We recommend, in general, that the facilitator impose a standard of "good enough" for norm writing.

Steps

1. Brainstorming. The facilitator encourages the group to brainstorm all possible norms, and lists the offerings for all to see. But the process begins with a few moments of silence as people consider what they want to offer. The facilitator also participates in the brainstorming, adding whatever seems lacking from the emerging list—for example, "We want to create a place that is safe enough in order for us to endure discomfort," or "We want to be allowed to take a risk."
2. *Discussion.* The facilitator says, "So far this is just a brainstormed list—we have not yet agreed to it. Is there something that needs discussion, that you want to question?"
3. *Synthesis.* In a transparent way—that is, voicing his or her deliberations aloud—the facilitator synthesizes and fine-tunes: "I think that what I'm hearing is that we want to be assured that good judgment will prevail. There can be situations where a phone must be left on, and we don't want to prevent that when needed. On the other hand, we don't want a bunch of phones ringing. So maybe the norm should be that we will only leave phones on when our judgment tells us we must. This is good. I was going to just say 'No phones,' but this is much better."
4. *Consensus.* Noting that consensus means that all group members can live with and support the norms, the facilitator moves the group to affirm the list.

Facilitation Tips

The facilitator should point out to the group that we call these things "norms" rather than "rules" to suggest their provisional status. Norms can be changed at any time. Indeed, norms that are intended to serve the group over a period of time are useful only if they are revisited with some regularity. Therefore, it is good to reflect on them from time to time: "How are we doing with our norms?" Meanwhile, for groups that meet over time, the chart paper or a print-out or jump drive with the norms can be carried over from meeting to meeting. Reviewing how the norms worked can be a good closing activity.

Variation

When time is really short, the facilitator can provide a list of norms for the group's consideration. Two excellent facilitators we know, Daniel Baron and Gene Thompson-Grove, sometimes say: "There is only one norm: If you think it, say it. If you wonder it, ask it."

Provocative Prompts

Nancy Mohr often used quotations from expert outsiders to stimulate insider discussions. The power of quotations in this regard comes not just from what they say about a topic at hand, but also from the fact that they say different things—a fact made obvious in what one selects and how one arrays the selections. If even experts disagree, others feel safer in owning up to and expressing their own disagreements.

Alan Dichter has often used short provocative quotations to stimulate discussions of such topics as working toward equity in education, the purpose of teachers' studying student work, the role of standards in teaching and learning, and the things that beginning teachers most need to learn.

Rather than presenting one way of using an array of contrasting quotations below, we alter our typical format to describe several simple protocols for doing so. Each one should be followed up by an open discussion or a go-round.

Purpose

The purpose of the protocols is to infuse a conversation about a particular topic with a quick and contrasting set of viewpoints on it—viewpoints that participants in a learning group can use to help elicit, shape, and reexamine their own perspectives and attitudes. They are often used as a way into a complex issue that is then treated in a more comprehensive way.

Details

The usefulness of these protocols depends on the provocation in the quotations themselves and in the contrast among them. The facilitator selects the quotations ahead of time and has them ready to distribute in the format desired. Time can vary to suit circumstances, but a quick pace is usually advantageous here. In online or blended environments, recorded voices might substitute for written quotations.

Protocol Versions

1. The facilitator distributes a page or two with all quotations and their sources listed. Each participant chooses one quotation and shares in a go-round why he or she chose it.
2. The facilitator distributes a page or two with all quotations and their sources listed, then invites each member of the group to choose one quotation that provokes him or her to think differently about the topic at hand and write briefly an account of the difference. Then the facilitator asks all members to share what they have written with a partner, with the partners reflecting back in their own words what they think the difference means. This can be done with several changes of partners.
3. The facilitator prepares the quotations on individual strips of paper, then hands out the strips randomly to everybody in the group. Each person reads the quotation he or she gets and responds to it on the spot. This obviously requires having one quotation for each person in the group.
4. The facilitator prepares the quotations on individual strips of paper, and hands out the strips randomly to every participant. The participants then walk about the room, and as they bump into each other, they argue with each other about their prompts—"believing" in their own, and "doubting" the other's.
5. The facilitator writes or prints the quotations on large chart paper and tapes the paper to the walls of a room or corridor. Participants, using Post-its, place comments and questions, as they choose, on each of the quotations.
6. After providing some examples, the facilitator invites participants to search the Internet for two contrasting provocative prompts and post the results—for example, in a shared Google doc. This jointly produced trove of prompts then becomes the text for any of the versions above.

Facilitation Tips

Each of the simple protocols described above can run for variable amounts of time, though the facilitator should be aware that extremely engaging discussion often results from Provocative Prompts, and sticking to the stated time frame can require one's full attention.

Variations

At the end of an extended exploration of a topic by a learning group—or along the way—participants can add to the quotation collection that got them started, and they can even engage in an additional round of Provocative Prompts as a way of bringing closure. In this round, they might try to find one quote each to connect (more or less exactly) to the expressions "I used to believe . . ." and "Now I believe . . ."

A group that uses the Final Word protocol (see Chapter 5) over the course of an extended period of time can collect the text passages highlighted by participants for that protocol and recycle them for this one.

Marvin's Model

We learned this protocol years ago from a professor at a midwestern university who used it routinely in his classes. All we can remember now is his first name, which has stuck to the protocol in the many contexts where it is now used.

Purpose

The purpose of this protocol is to facilitate rapid communication about a topic at hand among a large group of people, or to get many points of view in play quickly without engaging in dialogue. This can be used to open or close a meeting, or on occasion to intervene.

Steps

1. *Introduction.* The facilitator asks the large group to break into subgroups of five to seven members, then instructs the subgroups as follows: "When I ask a question, I will give you 30 seconds to think, and then each member of your group will answer quickly, in turn. Each will get exactly 30 seconds to answer. As each member speaks, the others listen silently. No one responds to anyone else's answer."

2. *Questions.* The facilitator poses a series of questions, for example, "What's the first thing you think about when I say mathematics [or writing, or science]?" "What do you think about when it comes to the teaching of mathematics [writing, science]?" "How about the assessment of learning in mathematics [writing, science]?"

3. *Debriefing.* Following several questions, the facilitator debriefs the group: "What has the group learned from this first exploration of the topic at hand? What, if anything, do members think we might have to unlearn?"

Facilitation Tips

Some participants will be unable to form an answer to some questions in the time provided. The facilitator should allow for this, granting permission to take a pass. Later, the facilitator can point out that both the answers and the passes may provide insight for the debriefing.

Variations

Besides being used as an opener, Marvin's Model can be used as a way of generating spontaneous responses to a speaker or a reading, responses that can then be followed up in a discussion. It can also be used in closing, as a way to share a lot of complex reaction in a relatively short amount of time.

CHAPTER 3

Working on Practice

Professional educators solve problems of practice continually, often hundreds in a single day. We sometimes solve them in ways that seem definitive, as when, for example, we finally decide which text we'll adopt for a particular course, or finally figure out a good fourth-grade placement for Jason, or discover a new way to help Olivia learn to write better. Still, we are not surprised when our "definitive" solutions come undone, or when they generate one or more other problems. In a famous essay in the *Harvard Educational Review*, Magdalene Lampert (1985) proposes that most of the problems we confront in practice are really dilemmas. They present options that seem irreconcilable: whether to punish or forgive, whether to press all the way or yield, whether to believe or to doubt, whether to insist on the detail or overlook it, and so on. In practice, though, the educator manages to reconcile the irreconcilable by alternating emphases—pressing to a point and then yielding, being tough in public and forgiving in private. Even as he or she manages the problems in this way, however, the teacher—or principal or dean—is chronically aware that one day's wise move may be another day's foolish one, and that either day's move may come to seem either wise or foolish given a certain shift of context.

Thus all of us find ourselves solving problems provisionally, and again and again. This inescapable condition of our work can make us feel like Sisyphus rolling his rock up the hill. In such circumstances we may run low on creative approaches even while the problems never run low on novel ways of presenting themselves. Meanwhile, the people on whose behalf we must address the problems come and go endlessly, blithely ignorant of the troubles they cause. Who is the teacher who has not on occasion thought, "Oh, no, another group of eighth graders!" Who is the dean who has not thought, "When will this faculty ever get it?"

In this chapter we present eight protocols that help educators sustain courage in the face of predictably chronic problems. They all involve framing some of the myriad problems of practice for collegial review. The point of the review is to gain the benefit of others' perspectives and thereby inform one's own, to draw on others' creative resources and thereby replenish one's own, and to experience in the process the encouraging effects of sharing one's burdens for an hour or so. The first protocol in the chapter is one we explored in Chapter 1, the Tuning Protocol, and is seminal in a number of respects—including in its lending the word *protocol* to a whole class of learning tools. It is seminal also in its adaptability. Indeed, the last protocol in this chapter, the Peer Review Protocol, is one of its many adaptations. The five protocols that follow the Tuning Protocol enable colleagues, fellow students, or others to *consult* with each other about practical problems by means of questioning, describing, uncovering, delving, and speculating. We use the word *consult* to signal the seminal impact of the Consultancy protocol, also explored in Chapter 1. Then the next-to-last protocol in the chapter involves a quintessential problem of practice—namely, the creation of goal-oriented strategies.

Tuning Protocol

The Tuning Protocol and adaptations of it are often used when professional educators study student work together (Allen, 1998; Blythe et al., 1999/2007). However, the roots of the protocol are in the collaborative exploration of educators' problems. It was originally designed as a way to gain helpful feedback on a small set of high school redesign efforts in progress within the Coalition of Essential Schools (CES). The IBM Corporation, which had funded the efforts, invited the schools to present on their progress. CES staff wanted to avoid two possible perils in such a meeting—that the presenters might "put on a show" rather than use the presentation as an opportunity to get valuable feedback, and that the feedback might be overly critical.

Purpose

As a problem-solving tool, the Tuning Protocol aims to ensure that educators receive honest, direct, and respectful feedback on the problems they present, and that they gain as well the opportunity to reflect on the feedback. It also aims to help all participants "tune up" their values through contact with others' diverse and candid perspectives. It forces presenters to frame a particular problem from the hundreds they might select, and to collect and present evidence that bears on the problem. It orients their colleagues to examine both the problem and the evidence from both *warm*—or appreciative—perspectives and *cool*—or critical—ones too.

Details

The Tuning Protocol takes 45 minutes to an hour or more, depending on such factors as the number of people involved and the complexity of what is presented for tuning. In the steps below, we provide timing guidelines for an hour-long session, which is common. Usually 6 to 12 participants are involved, though the protocol is sometimes used by groups as large as 30. Presenters might share relevant supporting materials, which may include documents in paper or video format.

Steps

1. *Introduction*. The facilitator briefly introduces the protocol goals and norms and distributes a copy of the steps. (5 minutes)
2. *Presentation*. The presenter shares the problem, or a draft of a plan currently under development, and provides relevant information about efforts to date. The presenter may also highlight particular questions that he or she would like the respondents to address, drawing on documents as appropriate to support the presentation. During this step, respondents may not speak. (15 minutes)
3. *Response*. Respondents note their warm and cool reactions to what the presenter has said. Warm reactions emphasize the strength of the presenter's views of the problem and his or her particular approaches to solving it. Cool reactions emphasize problematic aspects of these. Often cool reactions come in the form of questions: "I'm wondering why you chose to . . ." or "I'm curious about your interpretation of the parental reaction. Could you say more?" During this step, the presenter may not speak. He or she is encouraged instead to take notes, and in the process to consider which responses to comment on and which to let pass. In some versions of the Tuning Protocol, participants are invited to offer warm reactions first, then cool. In other versions, participants are encouraged to mix warm and cool (though never in the same response). (15 minutes)
4. *Reaction*. The presenter reacts to any responses he or she chooses to react to. The presenter is reminded that the response is not meant to answer questions but to talk about her or his thinking. During this step, respondents may not speak. (10 minutes)
5. *Conversation*. Presenter and respondents engage in open conversation. (10 minutes)
6. *Debriefing*. Participants reflect on the process and explore ways to use the protocol in other situations. The facilitator may ask, "How did it feel hearing warm and cool feedback? How did it feel not being able to respond to the feedback? How can you apply this protocol in your ordinary work?" (5 minutes)

Facilitation Tips

Each step of the protocol requires a prespecified allotment of time (though not necessarily those suggested above). The facilitator must therefore watch the clock. In some versions of the protocol, facilitators simply facilitate. In other versions, they are permitted to offer responses, typically to redress an imbalance between warm and cool comments. In such cases, however, facilitators must make sure that they do not dominate. A good rule of thumb in this regard is that the facilitator should never be the first to offer either a warm or a cool comment (though he or she may ask for someone else to do so). Another is that he or she should refrain from offering more than one of each unless absolutely necessary to redress an imbalance.

The facilitator should advise the presenter to respond to the warm as well as the cool reactions. Indeed, the facilitator should take care throughout the protocol—in his or her introductory remarks and responses—to suggest that warm reactions are not simply a prologue to cool ones, that both warm and cool reactions deserve thoughtful attention from presenter and respondents.

The facilitator should be prepared to interrupt tactfully when a participant violates the protocol—for example, by speaking out of turn, or by mixing warm and cool.

Variation

In some versions of the protocol there is an added step following the presentation. Here respondents ask "clarifying questions." The facilitator must ensure that these do not cross the boundary into warm or cool reactions. He or she may say, for example, that a particular clarifying question might be better saved for the next round.

With small groups and abbreviated timing, each participant can have his or her presentation—that is, problem statement and concerns—"tuned" in less than an hour. In this fashion, the Tuning Protocol can be used in classrooms as a device whereby students offer each other feedback on their work.

We have also sometimes used the Tuning Protocol as a feedback mechanism following lengthy professional retreats, where the presentation is the retreat itself and the problem is how to improve the format for the next time. Hearing the reaction by retreat organizers provides a wonderful opportunity for transparency and serves to help participants increase their sophistication regarding retreat design.

Consultancy

This protocol was developed by Gene Thompson-Grove, Paula Evans, and Faith Dunne in their work at the Coalition of Essential Schools and the Annenberg Institute for School Reform at Brown University. In Chapter 1, we explored the Consultancy as one of three seminal protocols, whose basic elements help define what protocols are and do. Here we provide step-by-step instructions.

Purpose

The Consultancy protocol has two main purposes: to develop participants' capacity to see and describe the dilemmas that are the essential material of their work, and to help each other understand and deal with them.

Details

The key component of a Consultancy is the thoughtful preparation for presentation by a colleague—or stranger—of a dilemma that genuinely matters to him or her. The Consultancy group is typically a small and intimate one—from three to six or seven. However, larger groups can easily subdivide into Consultancy groups.

Steps

1. *Framing the dilemma.* The presenter offers an overview of a dilemma from his or her practice. The overview presents key features, but is not an exhaustive account. In effect, it depends on the consultants' capacity to expand it through questions and inference. In this step, the presenter may also offer artifacts—for example, student work. (10 minutes or longer if there are artifacts)
2. *Clarifying questions.* Consultants ask questions that aim to elicit some details that they think they need in order to offer better consultation. These questions often have one- or two-word responses. (5 minutes)
3. *Probing questions.* Consultants ask questions that they hope will provoke deeper thinking by the presenter about the dilemma, and possible paths toward resolution. The presenter responds to the questions as well as he or she can, though sometimes a probing question might ask the presenter to see the dilemma in such a novel way that the response is simply, "I never thought about it that way." (10 minutes)

4. *Discussion.* In this step, the consultants discuss what they have heard, and what they have not heard. They talk about assumptions underlying the dilemma and reflect on what they might do were they in the presenter's shoes. (15 minutes)
5. *Presenter's reflection.* Here the presenter reflects on what he or she has learned from the consultancy. The presenter should not feel compelled to respond to everything that is said. (5 minutes)
6. *Debrief the Consultancy process.* The group—presenter, facilitator, and consultants—talk about the process, so as to improve it next time. (5 minutes)

Facilitator Tips

Gene Thompson-Grove urges facilitators of this protocol to resist in both Steps 3 and 4 the temptation among consultants to "solve the problem" or presume to lead the presenter to "solve the problem." Giving into this temptation is never helpful, she says, because the presenter knows far better that the consultants the complexities involved. She also suggests that in Step 5, the facilitator should caution against using the time to clarify details. "We know we got some things wrong," he or she might say to the presenter, "but use this time to think aloud about what resonates for you."

Descriptive Consultancy

In this substantial variation of the Consultancy, the presenter gains the opportunity of learning how others frame his or her dilemma. Nancy Mohr, who designed the protocol, used it especially to help groups of educators become facilitative leaders. Over a series of meetings these educators would present a number of dilemmas to each other for descriptive consultation. In the process they not only obtained better perspectives on their own problems, but became better consultants.

Purpose

As with the simple Consultancy, the Descriptive Consultancy has two purposes: helping a practitioner think through a dilemma that he or she presents, and expanding his or her power to address it. Both involve learning how to engage in what many scholars in the social sciences call "reframing" or "frame reflection." These scholars include Erving Goffman (1974), Donald Schön and Martin Rein (1994), Lee Bolman and Terry Deal (1997), and George Lakoff (2002, 2004).

Details

The protocol requires approximately 1 hour for the exploration of each dilemma, though overall times vary depending on the number of participants. The setting typically involves either one group of 10 to 12 or smaller groups of 3 to 5 participants each, meeting in a space where multiple conversations can be carried on simultaneously. Smaller groups—using a more constrained time frame—might consult on all its members' dilemmas in turn.

Steps

1. *Presentation.* The presenting group member describes the dilemma, laying out its different dimensions as he or she sees them, including previous attempts to address it if relevant. (10 minutes)
2. *Clarifying questions.* Other members of the group (acting in the role of consultants) ask questions designed to elicit information the consultants think they need in order to consult more effectively. (5 minutes)
3. *Reflecting back descriptively.* The presenter is silent while each of the consultants *describes* the content of the presentation beginning with the facilitator's prompt, "What did you hear in this presentation?" The facilitator then adds prompts to spur additional go-rounds in order to ensure the fullest possible description of the problem and its complexities. Such prompts might include: "What seems important to the presenter?" "What if anything surprised you?" and "What does this problem seem to be about?" Participants in the go-rounds are asked to pass if their reflection has already been offered by someone else. (10–15 minutes)
4. *Response.* The presenter briefly responds to the consultants' expressed understandings of the problem and provides further clarification of the problem as needed. (5 minutes)
5. *Brainstorming.* The presenter is again silent while the consultants brainstorm possible solutions or next steps, saying things like this: "What if . . . ?" "Have you thought about . . . ?" This step often takes the form of open conversation among the consultants, and sometimes in the third person (as if the presenter were not in the same room). This trick often helps the presenter to listen more fully and the consultants to speak more freely. (10–15 minutes)
6. *Response.* The presenter responds again, this time to answer any questions that have arisen in the brainstorming, and to acknowledge

any shifts in how he or she now views the problem. Here the presenter does not so much answer the group's questions as present his or her new insights gained through listening. (5 minutes)

7. *Debriefing.* The facilitator asks participants about their roles: "How did it feel to be the presenter? How did it feel to be the consultant?" The facilitator ends with, "Sometimes people other than the presenter learn something important from a Descriptive Consultancy—something useful in their own context. Does anyone have something to share along those lines?" (5 minutes)

Facilitation Tips

When Descriptive Consultancy is conducted in multiple small groups, the facilitator oversees the process as a whole, having first modeled it by allowing participants to observe an abbreviated or full version. During the process, the facilitator should monitor the groups' use of the steps, not hesitating to intervene if they are not being followed. In explaining and monitoring, the facilitator should especially emphasize the importance of Step 3—reflecting back a description, rather than making a judgment or proposing a solution. The watch phrase should be, "No rush to advice before it's time." This is a delicate step for the facilitator, who must gently nudge the group to remain descriptive.

The facilitator should also emphasize Step 4, which involves the presenter's listening to the way the consultants frame the problem. "The reason we reflect back," the facilitator might tell the group, "and listen carefully to the reflections, is to acknowledge that people inevitably have different takes on a complex problem. The power of Descriptive Consultancy is in learning from these different takes." The facilitator may ask the presenter at the end of Step 4 if he or she wants to reframe or restate the problem at this time.

Variation

Sometimes it is useful for a team to present a problem for consultation. This has the benefit for the team—say, a leadership group at a college—to become clearer about the problem as they think through how to present it.

Issaquah Coaching Protocol

This protocol was developed by Deb Bambino, Daniel Baron, and Nancy Mohr, who first used it at a retreat for coaches of schools affiliated with the Small Schools Collaborative in Washington State. The retreat took place in Issaquah State Park, hence the name. Like the Descriptive Consultancy, this is a substantial variation of the Consultancy protocol. The difference is the strong emphasis here on mimicking the successive moves of a coach or consultant, for example:

- *Elicit facts:* "Tell us what happened. What's the situation?"
- *Listen actively and reflect back:* "What I hear you say is . . ."
- *Interpret:* "What I think this means is . . ."
- *Check-in:* "Am I getting it right? Is what I'm saying making sense?"
- *Probe:* "Some additional questions I now have for you to think about are . . ."
- *Connect/extend:* "Ideas this brings to mind for me are . . ."
- *Elicit response:* "What do you think you will do about this situation?"

Purpose

Because this protocol models a developmentally appropriate order for questioning in coaching and consulting situations, it can be especially useful for educators whose roles involve such situations.

Details

The running time for this protocol is approximately an hour. The ideal group size is 10 to 15. If the group is larger, the facilitator should divide it into small groups of 3 to 4 participants each. These groups then respond *as groups* to each of the protocol's prompts, after a brief caucus and through spokespeople.

Steps

1. *Presentation.* A participant presents a problem that he or she has been working on. It must be real rather than simulated, and still be unresolved. The consultants are silent in this step. (10 minutes)
2. *Clarifying questions.* These questions are for information only, to help the consultants understand the problem more fully. (5 minutes)
3. *Active listening/reflecting back.* In a go-round, each consultant briefly restates the problem in consulting terms, prefaced by such remarks as: "I hear you say . . ." "What I'm hearing is . . ." Consultants refrain from interpretation or speculation. The facilitator tells them that the purpose of this step is not only to understand the presentation better, but to help the presenter learn from others' interpretations of what he or she has said, and to correct misinterpretations. The presenter is silent in this step. (5 minutes)

4. *Check-in.* The facilitator asks the presenter, "Quickly, are we hearing you correctly? If not, what would you change/add?" Presenter responds. (2 minutes)

5. *Interpretive listening/reflecting back.* Consultants respond in a go-round to the following prompt: "What I think is going on in this problem is . . ." Presenter is silent. (10 minutes)

6. Check-in again. The facilitator prompts the presenter, "How does our thinking sound to you? Does it make sense?" Presenter responds. (5 minutes)

7. *Probing questions.* These are questions intended to get the presenter to think more deeply about the dilemma or problem presented. The presenter who remains silent in this step is advised not to answer them, but to use them instead to push his or her own thinking. The facilitator cautions the consultants not to ask leading questions, ones tailored to get the presenter to think as they do. In this step, some facilitators allow time for the consultants to prepare their questions (10 minutes including preparation time)

8. *Response.* Here the presenter is asked simply whether any of the probing questions made him or her think differently about the dilemma or problem. The facilitator reminds everyone that the point of this step is not to answer the questions, but just to help the consultants gain more access to the presenter's thoughts on the problem. (5 minutes)

9. *Suggestions.* Finally, and only if the presenter agrees that suggestions are desired, consultants may offer some, again in a consulting framework: "What if you . . . ?" "Have you thought about . . . ?" (5 minutes)

10. *Response.* The presenter responds with thoughts about "next steps"—concrete, long- and short-term steps that now seem possible. (2 minutes)

11. *Debriefing.* This starts with the presenter; then all participants may join in. The facilitator prompts with such questions as these: What was it like to go through these steps? Which kind of question was most useful/least useful? Could the process follow a different order and work better? How does this relate to your work in the field? (5 minutes)

Facilitation Tips

The facilitator should make it clear that the purpose of this consultation is to provide the kind of help that is wanted. Some people want advice (though typically only after they feel fully heard in their account of the problem), while others prefer merely to have their thinking pushed.

To achieve the larger purpose of this protocol (beyond helping someone work through a problem), the facilitator should periodically call attention to the fact that the protocol simulates a consulting situation. For example, the facilitator might remind a "consultant" to use a "consulting voice."

Peeling the Onion

In her work consulting with groups of educators, Nancy Mohr discovered that the questions participants brought to such activities as the Descriptive Consultancy were often "surface" ones. By the end of the consultation, everyone would discover that the starting question was not the "real" one. She developed this protocol to deal explicitly with this phenomenon.

Purpose

Peeling the Onion provides a structured way to develop an appreciation for the complexity of a problem. It aims to circumvent the inclination of many groups to start out immediately "solving" a problem at hand (which may not be the real problem at all).

Details

The protocol takes approximately 40 minutes and is best done in a group of 10 to 12 members.

Steps

1. *Sharing the problem.* Someone agrees to share a problem that he or she needs help with. (5 minutes)
2. *Clarifying questions.* Only clarifying questions may be asked—ones that elicit brief additional explanation. (3 minutes)
3. *Active listening.* The facilitator leads a go-round in which everyone completes the statement: "I understand the problem to be . . ." The presenter stays silent and takes notes. (10 minutes)
4. *Peeling/probing.* The facilitator leads another go-round in which everyone gets to pose additional questions raised by having heard the first round. (10 minutes)
5. *Response.* The facilitator invites a response from the presenter as follows: "Having heard these questions, please share any new thoughts about the problem you presented." (5 minutes)
6. *Open conversation.* The group is invited to have an open conversation. (5 minutes)

7. *Debriefing.* The facilitator prompts: "How was this like peeling an onion? What other 'onions' do you imagine peeling?" (2 minutes)

Facilitation Tips

The facilitator should start by saying something like the following: "Most of us are eager to solve problems before we truly understand their depth. This protocol is designed to help us peel away the layers in order to see that most problems are not simple, and they require more than our initial take on what should be done."

The facilitator should keep to the times strictly and gently correct participants whenever they *solve* rather than *peel*.

Success Analysis Protocol

Educators can gain much by collaboratively analyzing past experiences of failure—when the plan fell apart, when the students' reactions were not at all what was expected, and so on. However, the point of this protocol, designed by Daniel Baron, is to give equal attention to past experiences of success. Here the "problem of practice" is to understand more fully in such cases why things go right. This is especially important because most cases of success in professional practice are examples of successful problem solving.

One might think that examining success is easier than examining failure, and that people might take more readily to the former. However, it turns out to be rather more difficult in practice. Participants may be unsure that their sense of success will match others', and may thus spend unnecessary energy on providing evidence of success. Or they may find it hard to position themselves as contributors to success for fear of seeming self-congratulatory. Facilitators should acknowledge that these are common problems by way of urging participants to get over them.

Purpose

The purpose of the Success Analysis Protocol is to engage colleagues in collaborative analysis of cases from practice in order to understand the circumstances, contributions, and actions that make them successful ones, and then to apply this understanding to future practice.

Details

Twelve to 30 participants work in small groups of 3 to 6. Chart paper or electronic means of recording responses should be available. Participants need to be able to take notes. The size of the small groups will determine the length of the activity, since all participants should present.

Steps

1. *Preparing a case.* Participants are asked to reflect on and write individually (in the form of notes for themselves) a short case describing one area where they are finding success or making progress in practice. The case should include specific details concerning their own involvement in it—what they did that may have contributed to its success. It should also account for other factors that may underlie the success, including any favorable conditions present. This step may be done in advance of the meeting. (10 minutes)
2. *Sharing.* In the small groups, the first person shares orally his or her case of successful practice, while the others take notes. (5 minutes)
3. *Analysis and discussion.* The group reflects on the success. Participants offer their own insights into what made this case of practice successful. They discuss specifically what they think the presenter may have done to contribute to success, and they also name what they take to be other factors involved. The presenter is encouraged to participate and is prodded through questioning. (5 minutes)
4. *Repeating the pattern.* Repeat Steps 2 and 3 for each member of the group.
5. *Compilation.* The group then compiles on chart paper or via laptop if a projector is available a list of specific successful behaviors and underlying principles that seem characteristic of the cases presented. (5 minutes)
6. *Reporting out.* If there are multiple small groups, the groups report out in some way, for example, by means of posting lists around the room and "gallery walking" to read all the lists, or by means of projecting their lists and citing highlights. (5 minutes)
7. *Discussion.* The facilitator prompts a general discussion with the questions, "Do the lists have elements in common? Do any contain behaviors or underlying principles that surprised you?"(10 minutes)
8. *Debriefing.* Still in the large group, the facilitator asks, "How might we apply what we have learned in this protocol to other parts of our work? How might students use this protocol or a variation of it to reflect on their work?"

Facilitation Tips

There is a tendency for presenters to spend time providing evidence that the case presented was indeed a case of success. Facilitators need to remind them that they don't need to prove success, but that they do need to be explicit about what they (and others) contributed to success.

If participants are asked to prepare their cases of success in advance, the facilitator should give them a few minutes to review their notes. This will ensure that people are focused, and provide those who did not actually prepare a chance to develop their thinking.

It sometimes helps people new to this protocol to have the facilitator join in, presenting a case also—perhaps a case of successful facilitation. This can be done in fishbowl fashion, with one small group participating and the others observing. It may also help beginners if the facilitator uses the expression "stories of success" instead of "cases of success."

When participants overgeneralize and depersonalize—as, for example, "We had a small group of teachers meeting to review our new homework policy"—the facilitator should remind them to say what they themselves contributed. This helps demystify success.

Variation

The facilitator may ask that everyone focus on the same theme—for example, a successful staff meeting, a successful peer observation, or a successful project design. In such cases, small groups compile a composite list and report out. The facilitator then leads a general discussion about common successful practices.

Stuff and Vision Protocol

This protocol is designed to help teachers, teams of teachers, or student teachers use material they have uncovered or amassed in order to create well-targeted lesson plans or curriculum units. Its premise is that good teaching is a combination of the right *stuff* and the right *vision*. The stuff might be concrete material of varying dimensions: contrasting political cartoons clipped from the week's news; data sets downloaded from the U.S. Census Bureau or any number of other websites; historical maps or other documents found at the Library of Congress website; or poems that have been copied or downloaded. Clearly, the Internet makes finding good stuff easy. But teaching well means using stuff purposefully, that is, with a set of explicit learning goals in mind—a vision of what students might do with political cartoons (reading them, mimicking them) and also of what they might thereby learn. Vision concerns, for example, what they will understand of how political cartoons work rhetorically and how this will scaffold their growing ability to make good arguments themselves.

The name of this protocol is intended to project a tone in its use. While planning thoughtful lessons and using good materials are serious objectives, the success of this protocol depends on a facilitator's light-handed touch and on a culture among participants of keeping options open and details unpinned.

Purpose

The purpose of this protocol is to assist teachers and student teachers to plan resourceful and ambitious lessons and units.

Details

The protocol is designed to take approximately 1 hour, with 10 or fewer teachers participating. Members of a team might take turns facilitating and presenting. If a group of four teachers meets weekly, for example, each might agree to facilitate once a month and present once a month.

Steps

1. *Introduction.* The facilitator reviews the steps of the protocol. (2 minutes)
2. *Vision input.* A participant presents a "vision" to his or her colleagues. The vision might be based on some document with which they are already quite familiar: the Common Core Standards for Mathematics, the state social studies standards for middle school, the grade-level goals the colleagues are all working toward, the aims of next month's collective unit that they have already discussed, and so on. And the presenter should have copies of this document on hand. The vision itself is an image of a performance goal fulfilled. Vague and general description is fine here—even preferred. For example, a presenter might say, "I see my students having written fabulous research papers that are original and carefully written, and then presenting these papers to each other, and getting lots of questions that they answer with a real sense of expertise." (5 minutes)
3. *Vision go-round.* Each of the participants briefly answers the question, "What comes to my mind when I think about this vision?" (30 seconds each)
4. *Stuff input.* The presenter must "show" as well as "tell"—that is, have something to pass out, pin to the wall, project on the screen, and so on. The emphasis of the presentation is on *possibility.* The

presenter should *not* present any teaching plans (though he or she doubtlessly has some in mind). The point is to invite design possibilities that the presenter has not already considered. (5–10 minutes)

5. *Questions.* Colleagues ask questions to help the presenter get clearer about what he or she finds appealing in the stuff, and what connections the presenter finds between stuff and vision. Questions should be genuinely open-ended, not evaluative comments in disguise. During this time the presenter stays silent, taking notes on what the colleagues ask. (10 minutes)

6. *Response.* The presenter has a chance to respond to any of the questions he or she chooses. (2 minutes)

7. *Designing on the spot.* Taking turns in a go-round, each of the members of the group (including the facilitator and ending with the presenter) offers a possible design linking stuff and vision. The designs should be still inchoate—invitations to further imagining. Indeed, the designs may well be merely design elements. Thus a participant might say on his or her turn: "I don't have a full-blown design in mind yet, but one thing I know is that you should make the articles on Guatemala the centerpiece—let assignments lead up to that and radiate off that." Members may not repeat what another person says or respond to other speakers, but must challenge themselves to offer yet another possible design, or to build on another's design element. Every member must say something in a spirit of joint ownership. The facilitator might say, "As if this were our design, we're all working hard here to realize a set of creative and functional plans." (10–15 minutes)

8. *Open conversation.* Everyone in the group has a chance to comment on or ask questions about any of the possibilities raised in the previous round. (10 minutes)

9. *Reflection.* The presenter ends the session by saying how, if at all, he or she has become clearer about what to do next. Typically, he or she is still uncertain of the final design, but excited by the new possibilities that have been generated and eager to take it from there. (2 minutes)

Facilitation Tips

The facilitator should strive to keep the tone light—about possibility, not polish. This will lower the stakes for the presenter, as well as for the colleagues' brainstorming in Step 7.

In Step 7 the facilitator might choose to go first and model for the others how to do this step, referring directly to elements of the vision. Between Steps 6 and 7, depending on the experience and comfort level of the group as well as the time available, the facilitator might add a "doodling" step—5 minutes for private designing. If the group does not have a whole hour to spend together, the steps and times can be compressed.

Variations

This protocol can easily be used in combination with *Japanese lesson study,* a collaborative planning process in which one or more members of the team go on to construct a lesson or unit on behalf of the team. One member then pilot-teaches the lesson to the team for its feedback, and goes on to teach it to students with one or more other members observing. To learn more about Japanese lesson study see, for example, Sato (1992), Stigler and Hiebert (1999), Watanabe (2002), or McDonald et al. (2003).

Stuff and Vision also readily lends itself to online use—especially since much "stuff" comes originally from online sources. Thus presenters can simply refer their colleagues to "stuff URLs," and post their design ideas. For a sense of how protocols work in online settings, see the next protocol (as well as McDonald et al., 2012).

Peer Review Protocol (Online)

An adaptation of the Tuning Protocol, the Peer Review Protocol was originally designed by Joe McDonald and Nancy Mohr for the New York State Academy for Teaching and Learning, an early effort to encourage standards-based teaching through an exchange of exemplary units of instruction. Tuning determined what was exemplary—that is, a rubric-guided conversation among peers, involving warm and cool feedback. Developed before the widespread use of the Internet, these conversations happened in regional and statewide face-to-face meetings (McDonald et al., 2003).

In 2007, when Frank San Felice (who had worked with the Academy) developed with Harvey Newman the Partnership for Innovation in Compensation for Charter Schools (PICCS), he adapted the New York Peer Review Protocol to a new but related purpose. PICCS is a project of the Center for Educational Innovation-Public Education Association, one of the longest established school reform organizations in the United States. San Felice wanted to use peer review to enhance the instructional power and effectiveness of the new PICCS network of independent charter schools, now 22 schools in New York and New Jersey. His plan was implemented over the next several years, with help from the Metro Learning Communities project at NYU, and today many teachers from PICCS-affiliated schools undergo peer review. The process works as follows. First, schools practice peer review within internal professional learning communities, using peer feedback and student data to polish colleagues' teaching plans to high-quality levels. Then the best of these plans are peer-reviewed at the network level, and those selected by peers (who have themselves been favorably reviewed) are featured on the PICCS Network's intranet and could earn their creators a compensation bump. Like PICCS school-level peer reviews, PICCS network-level reviews happen mostly in face-to-face environments today, and are rich cross-school faculty development experiences—comparable to the experience a teacher might have attending and presenting at a professional meeting. Because the PICCS Network is now far-flung, however, and also because small charter schools cannot easily spare teachers to attend network-level peer reviews during the school day, PICCS has begun to experiment with online network-level peer review, and hopes to expand its use. Indeed, we believe that online peer review is likely to grow in the years ahead not only within PICCS, but within other school networks too. And for them, the PICCS online template seems a good model to adapt.

Purpose

Peer review can be used for many purposes, but the purpose we focus on here involves the identification and spread of exemplary instructional practices. The PICCS network uses peer review as a forum for exploring and developing best practices within member schools, and for scaling them up across the network.

Details

The PICCS network-level Peer Review Protocol focuses on a unit of instruction that has previously been reviewed at the school level, and contains certain required elements. In order to give readers sufficient context, we list these required elements below, though other networks will likely have other required elements.

- A graphic overview or narrative description of the unit that includes grade level and subject, instructional focus, and a timeline on which key elements are noted.
- The specific learning standards that the unit addresses.
- Data that characterize the students for whom the unit was developed in terms of previous achievement levels and relevant demographics (e.g., English language learner or special needs status).
- An instructional overview that situates the unit within the school's larger curriculum, identifies its major instructional strategies, assesses its suitability for differentiating instruction, and notes any special materials it may require (e.g., technology support).

- At least two lesson plans that bring the unit to life for the reviewers.
- An assessment plan that includes methods of assessment (e.g., observation with checklist, writing prompt, oral quiz), rubrics used, and three samples of actual assessed student work (captured, for example, in PDF or video).
- A reflection by the unit's developer(s) on the unit's overall strengths and challenges, as well as tips to other teachers who want to try it. The tips might include ideas of how to adapt the unit to other settings.

In this version of the protocol, the peer review is conducted in an asynchronous online format over 2 "online weeks," with the 1st week focused on presentation and the 2nd on feedback. An "online week," as we use the expression here and in *Going Online with Protocols* (McDonald et al., 2012), is a unit of asynchronous teaching and learning roughly equivalent in time scale to an actual week. The phrase is a useful reminder that in order to accommodate participants' diverse schedules, asynchronous online teaching and learning activity needs a longer window than its face-to-face counterpart (2 weeks in this case instead of 2 hours). The 2 asynchronous "weeks" are capped by a final synchronous meeting (e.g., via Google Livechat, Skype, FaceTime, or other video conferencing software). This provides the reviewers an opportunity to assess the suitability of the reviewed unit for online dissemination, and to prepare a written response for the presenter.

There are at least three reviewers involved in a PICCS network-level review (with at least one experienced at the standards level or content area of the presentation). One of the reviewers serves as facilitator and another as recorder. The reviewers are typically teachers who have themselves successfully presented at the network level.

Steps

1. *Presenter preparation.* For the presenter, a good deal of the challenge of peer review is in preparing for it. Reviewers need the support of colleagues at their school who formally (as in PICCS) or informally pre-review their work, and they often need a technology coach, too—for example, a colleague who is handy with graphics, and who is available to videotape elements of the presentation (e.g., the instructional overview, the reflection, or parts of the lesson plan or assessment plan). This is particularly important if the intent (as in PICCS) is to turn successfully reviewed work into digital products available for others to use.

2. *Facilitator preparation.* For the facilitator, the initial challenge is to ensure that both the presenter and the reviewers have made their

online "presence" known. A good way to do this is to send the facilitator a photo of themselves in whatever setting they will use to conduct the review—for example, their desk at school or at home—plus a paragraph about their own experiences in peer review, and some welcoming remarks to the presenter. The facilitator does the same. Then the facilitator prepares the online site with postings of these materials. PICCS uses the online platform Eduplanet21 (www.eduplanet21.com).

3. *Introduction.* The facilitator posts the steps of the protocol with deadlines for each step. He or she also posts a message designed to set a tone for the review. This is one that encourages a balance of appreciation and critique (warm and cool) and situates the review in the context of the network's efforts to create a supportive community of rich and rigorous instructional practice.

4. *Presentation and reviewers' questions.* The presenter posts the entire presentation (see list of required elements above) in various formats—including, for example, some PDFs, some scanned student work, and an introductory video. The facilitator asks all reviewers to respond within 1 online week with any clarifying questions they have (ones that they need answered in order to conduct a helpful review—for example, a question about the order of activities in the assessment plan, or about the presenter's priorities among the targeted learning standards).

5. *Presenter's response to questions.* The 1st online week ends with the presenter's posted response to the clarifying questions.

6. *Warm and cool feedback.* The 2nd online week begins with the posting by each reviewer in preassigned turns of warm feedback and cool feedback. The reviewer posts both kinds of feedback simultaneously but clearly labels the postings "Warm Feedback" and "Cool Feedback," with typically two or three comments for each. Warm comments are appreciative, while cool comments are critical. Both typically zero in on particular elements of the unit, though they sometimes refer to global features. Cool comments are often though not necessarily expressed as questions—for example, "Why did you choose to . . . ?" The facilitator assigns posting days to each reviewer in order to ensure that subsequent postings take account of previous ones, and that the feedback overall covers a lot of ground.

7. *Presenter's response to feedback.* The 2nd online week ends with the presenter's response to the feedback. The presenter may respond to any part of the feedback or all of it, as he or she chooses. The presenter also has the option of "extending" the "week" as needed in order to confer with colleagues before responding.

8. *Reviewers' conference.* In a final synchronous online meeting, the reviewers (absent the presenter) review the feedback and response, and decide whether the unit as presented is ready for replication. In doing this, they consult the PICCS Peer Review Rubric. If the unit is not yet considered ready for replication, they prepare an email message for the presenter concerning recommendations for revision and resubmission for review. If the unit is considered ready, however, they provide instructions for final submission and online publication.

Facilitation Tip

As the account of the Peer Review Protocol (Online) may suggest, facilitating protocols online is in many respects different from facilitating them face to face; it requires different kinds of planning and employs somewhat different moves. Readers who may want to try facilitating this or other online protocols should consult McDonald et al. (2012) for an extended discussion of these differences.

CHAPTER 4

Working for Change

A GROUP OF Connecticut teachers from the largely rural and poor northeast quadrant of the state formed a study group in the early 1990s. It was focused on sharing and exploring student work in light of the new Connecticut standards. The teachers planned to educate themselves about what these standards (and the assessments to follow) might mean for their teaching. At one point, the new teacher study group adopted a logo and motto, and ordered some sweatshirts with both emblazoned. The logo featured two isosceles triangles. The one with its base near the bottom of the sweatshirt, represented teaching practice. "Like a mountain," the teachers said, "difficult to move and hard to scale." The other, with its base toward the neckline represented the state's standards. "Like a dagger," they said, expressing their fear of the newness of standards in those days. These triangles overlapped near their apexes, forming a third geometric figure, a diamond-shaped one. This was shaded in the logo and inscribed with the group's motto "Work the diamond"—that is, the sometimes elusive space in which policy prescriptions and practical knowledge can mix creatively (McDonald, 2001).

If chapters had mottos, "Work the diamond" would be a good one for this chapter. All the protocols featured here aim to work toward change in the context of real practice and real constraints on practice. The first four protocols focus on student work, where the impact of practice and the resistances it encounters become most visible. The first of these is What Comes Up, a simple protocol with English roots that was designed expressly for the Connecticut teachers. It focuses on two or three pieces of student work, and uses these to elicit and explore a faculty's expectations of their students' work in general, as well as the complications of student learning that the work makes manifest. Next is Standards in Practice, the Education Trust's protocol. It powerfully juxtaposes teacher-generated assignments, the actual student work the assignments produced, and the demands of external standards—for example, the new Common Core State Standards (CCSS; see website at www.corestandards.org). Third is the Minnesota Slice (often called simply the Slice Protocol). It focuses a group of stakeholders (sometimes a mixed one—for example, of faculty and parents) on the ways in which their expectations for learning may or may not jibe with the actual work demands of an ordinary day in school—as viewed from the perspective of student work. The fourth protocol, the Shadow Protocol, does somewhat the same thing, though it focuses on just one student at a time who has for some reason proved puzzling to teachers, and on the learning strengths and weaknesses evident in his or her work.

An alternative motto for this chapter, which would also apply to all its protocols but especially well to the final four, is "Do what you mean to do." That's also the title of the first of these final four protocols. It searches out the predictable gaps that arise between what we mean to do when we try to make change and what we actually do. Seeing these gaps more clearly helps make change-minded practitioners smarter in their next steps. The New Design Protocol, which comes next, works on forestalling gaps by helping change agents clarify their intentions from the start and design change collaboratively. Meanwhile, the School Visit Protocol looks at gaps from the other end, namely, after they have formed. It does so with patient attention to the ways such gaps may be bridged. Finally, the last of the chapter's protocols—called What Do We Know? Suspect? Need to Find Out?—explores gaps as they may be revealed in arrays of data—for example, student test data.

What Comes Up

Simon Clements, a former member of Her Majesty's Inspectors of Schools (HMI) in England, invented this protocol for the benefit of the Connecticut teachers' study group described above, adapting it from the traditions of the HMI, where the examination of student work is considered a crucial source of evidence for judgments about school quality (Wilson, 1996). In its encouragement of perception and its press for deeper and deeper levels of it, this protocol shows the influence, too, of the seminal protocol, the Collaborative Assessment Conference (see Chapters 1 and 5).

Purpose

The Connecticut teachers asked Simon for a protocol they could use in short after-school faculty meetings, the kind that are often dominated by announcements and that seldom focus on teaching and learning. Thus the purpose of What Comes Up is subversive if also practical.

Details

This is a protocol for a 30- to 45-minute meeting of 6 to 20 people who already know one another well because they work in the same department or program. It works best when seats are arranged in a circle or around a conference table. It depends on the facilitator's having already obtained at least one and preferably two to three pieces of student work, freshly collected from one or more of the participants' classrooms, with each focused on a different subject and composed in a different medium. It is best to choose pieces that are intriguing for some reason: because they raise questions, seem ambiguous, or appear unconventional.

Steps

1. *Presentation.* The facilitator presents the first piece of student work. Depending on the kind of work it is, the facilitator may choose to read it aloud (a story or poem), to post it on the wall (a drawing), or to pass out copies (notes on a science problem). Participants attend quietly to the work—listening, looking, reading. (up to 5 minutes)
2. *Question.* The facilitator then asks the participants to consider the question, "What comes up for you when you examine this piece of work?" Participants take a few moments to consider the question.
3. *Round of response.* Beginning with whoever seems most ready to start, the facilitator calls on people in turn, going around the circle. Each responds to the question. No one may speak out of turn. No one may repeat an observation. Depending on how much interest has been stimulated and how many people there are in the group, the facilitator may choose to go one more round.
4. *Conversation.* The facilitator invites open conversation based on what the group has learned from the round(s).
5. *Repeat.* Time permitting, the facilitator introduces a new piece of work, and the process repeats.

Facilitation Tips

The facilitator seeks to create an unhurried, reflective space carved out of ordinary work life. The protocol presses for depth through the gamelike prohibition on repeating an observation. The facilitator should insist on the rules of the game, but lightheartedly, giving each turn-taker time to think up a new comment if time is needed.

Variation

One can cross this protocol with the Tuning Protocol and have a warm round followed by a cool round in response to the question, "What comes up for you in considering this piece of student work?" Warm comments are empathetic, appreciative. Cool comments are detached, comparative.

Standards in Practice

This protocol was developed by the Education Trust, which engages in a variety of activities ranging from policy advocacy to school-level support for instructional change. All its activities are in the service of ensuring that all children, though especially poor children of color, have the benefit of high-quality teaching. The protocol has its origin in the effort of the Education Trust to correct an early assumption of standards-based school reform—namely, that all educators need in order to teach all students accountably and effectively is a clear set of academic standards and high expectations. Standards by themselves offer insufficient guidance, the Trust argues. Teachers still have to make difficult decisions about what content to teach, and about how and when to teach it. Meanwhile, teaching side by side in many schools and districts are teachers who know their subject matter well and believe their students can learn at high levels, and teachers who are less knowledgeable and think their students less capable. One group may be skillful in designing and using rich and demanding teaching plans, and the other may be reliant on worksheets and simple recall questions. The Trust aimed to devise an intervention to turn this "side by side" into a collegial learning opportunity for teachers—one that spreads high-level learning to all their students. Standards in Practice (SIP) is the name of this intervention as well as the protocol that governs it. It involves examining teachers' work over time (in the form of the tasks and projects they assign to their students) to determine if the learning demands embedded within them actually jibe with the content and skills specified in state and national standards—e.g., the Common Core State Standards (CCSS; see website at www.corestandards.org).

SIP is based on three core beliefs:

1. Schools *can* make a difference in overcoming the possible negative effects of poverty and race on achievement.
2. Effective instruction takes more than just believing this is possible. It also takes knowledge of content, of pedagogy, and of students' backgrounds and cultures. And it requires careful thought and judgment on the part of teachers.
3. Effective instruction also demands ongoing reflection, analytic thinking, self-critique, collegial support, and a commitment to improvement.

Purpose

The purpose of SIP is to increase the rigor of teachers' assignments over time by aligning them with standards, and pressing toward increased student learning. At first, the protocol is usually used with assignments already given, but as groups of teachers use it continually, it often changes into a planning tool as well—an opportunity to test out new assignment ideas and tune them up before the students get them. It works not just with teacher-designed assignments but with assignments derived from any source: textbooks, school or district curricula, and so on.

Details

SIP is designed for teams of six to eight teachers who meet for at least one class period a week—preferably 90 minutes—or every 2 weeks if weekly meetings are impossible. Frequency is crucial. The Trust warns, based on the research it has conducted, that meeting only once a month is not effective. It also suggests that the interest and engagement of principals is very important.

SIP teams can be organized in several different ways. At the elementary level, they may be formed vertically (e.g., teachers from Grades 1 through 6) or horizontally (e.g., all those who teach Grade 4). At the secondary level, teams can be organized by subject matter (e.g., mathematics or English/ language arts teachers) or by teachers who all see the same students. What guides choice in both cases is the school's needs.

Steps

1. *Introduction of the assignment.* One teacher on the team brings copies of an assignment for each member of the team. The class set of student work that resulted from the assignment is tucked away at this point—saved for Step 5. The team examines the assignment in order to consider content and context. The facilitator asks team members as they read to think about the learning purpose of the assignment. The teacher who has brought the assignment does not present it in the ordinary way, however, but trusts the team's power to read, infer, and interpret. He or she merely offers bare contextual information—for example, when the assignment was given and whether it was an in-class or homework assignment.

2. *Assessment of learning goals.* Team members list what they take to be the required skills and knowledge needed to complete the assignment successfully. Does it require problem solving? Computation? High levels of inferential reading skill? Familiarity with technical terms? Writing nonnarrative texts? And so on. They may begin this list privately, but they end up with a collaboratively constructed one, whether on chart paper or computer projection. This step is crucial

for ensuring that the standards focus of Step 3 is appropriately grounded.

3. *Identification of applicable standards.* Next the team identifies the standards that seem especially to apply to this assignment. They refer to any standards important within the school, district, or state—including the literacy and math Common Core Standards. Each assignment must be viewed in light of at least one content standard—for example, in history—and one literacy standard—for example, in writing. If the team has difficulty matching the assignment with at least one content standard and at least one literacy standard, then it skips to Step 6.

4. *Development of a rough scoring guide.* Using a scale of 1–4 ("fails to meet standard" through "exceeds standard"), the team generates a rough diagnostic rubric or scoring guide for the assignment based on the applicable standards. The facilitator asks such questions as the following: "When students meet the standards on this assignment, what qualities might characterize their work? How about when they fail to meet standards? How about when they exceed standards?" In the process of developing the scoring guide, the team discusses the levels of complexity associated with the assignment and also begins to imagine varieties of student response to it. Coming to terms with both these dimensions of an assignment is crucial to improving it.

5. *Assessment of student work.* Using the rubric/scoring guide, each team member individually scores the student work that the presenting teacher has brought and now shares. Then the team shares their tallies. In the sharing they discuss discrepancies and try to reconcile them. If they cannot reach complete agreement, they settle on rough agreement: distinguishing between proficient (a score of 3 or 4) and not proficient (2 or 1).

6. *Using student work to plan assignment improvements.* This is the most important step of the protocol, which is why the Education Trust often calls SIP the "six-step conversation." New participants may think SIP is all about scoring student work, but this is merely a prelude to answering the question of whether a particular assignment is worth students' time and why. As part of this last step, participants examine this question. They look closely at the student work that resulted from the assignment, discuss what may account for its meeting standard or falling short of standard, and consider how the assignment may need to change. Teams that had to skip Steps 4 and 5 because they could not discern applicable standards in Step 3 may use this step to devise another assignment.

Facilitation Tips

The Education Trust recommends that SIP teams follow the SIP process faithfully for the first few months. Later, however, as collegial bonds form, SIP practices may usefully vary. The facilitator should look for signs at the end of the protocol that teachers feel mentally stretched, and that they have thought deeply about their work as teachers and their impact on all their students. These are good indicators of the need to vary or not.

Variations

As we suggested above, SIP can be useful in providing retrospective feedback on completed assignments or in tuning up future assignments, or both. So Steps 1–4 can serve as a planning tool, and Steps 5–6 can take account of the results. However, the Trust suggests that SIP should not be used as a planning tool until teachers are ready to replace their activities—that is, until they themselves are convinced based on retrospective work that their present assignments do not always work as they hoped they might.

Minnesota Slice

The Slice Protocol for studying student work was first used by the Bush Educational Leaders Program at the University of Minnesota in the early 1990s. Joe McDonald devised the protocol with help from Jean King and John Mauriel. Since then, it has migrated to many other contexts. In Minnesota it was always part of a larger inquiry focused on a question raised by a school or district. For example, one year a particular Minnesota school district wanted to know what teachers, students, parents, and other community members thought should be the purpose of education in their small town. So the Bush Fellows organized focus groups, conducted a phone survey, shadowed some students through an entire day of school, held a town meeting, and collected a "slice."

The word slice reflects the fact that the student work to be studied is a broad but still limited swath of work. In this same Minnesota district, for example, it consisted of all the work done by students between 12:00 noon one day and 3:00 p.m. the next day (including homework) in two kindergarten, second-grade, fourth-grade, and sixth-grade classes in each of two elementary schools, plus all of the work done within the same time span by 25 students per school (chosen randomly from each of three strata reflecting achievement levels) at both the middle school and high school. The elementary work was collected by the teachers. The middle school and high school work was collected by the students. Both teachers and students were encouraged to take photos of work that could not be collected (e.g., silent reading, group work, artwork, physical exercise). All the collected work was photocopied once names and other identifying characteristics were masked, and particular class sets (at the elementary level) and student sets (at the secondary level) were then assigned numbers. Photos were arranged separately.

Frequently, a slice (here we use lowercase to refer to the corpus of work collected rather than to the overall protocol) is less elaborate than it was in this Minnesota example. For example, it may not be part of a more elaborate inquiry involving other methods, and it may involve only one school rather than a whole district. For example, at University Neighborhood High School (UNHS), a small school on the Lower East Side of New York City, a slice consisted of the work done by 15 students over the course of a day and a half. The students were volunteers who received community service credit for their collection efforts. They represented a range of skill levels, but included a slightly higher proportion of special education students than are found in the school's population overall. One of the things the school was interested in learning from the slice was whether such students were being appropriately challenged.

Regardless of how elaborate it is, a slice once prepared becomes a "text" for discussion by a group of protocol participants. The participants may be limited to the school's faculty, as at UNHS, or may include outsiders, too, as in Minnesota, where parent leaders were also invited. Before proceeding with a reading and discussion of this text, the participants are advised to remember that any slice provides just a small window on the teaching and learning life of a community. Like all windows, it excludes from view far more than it includes.

Purpose

The purpose of the Slice Protocol is to help answer a question raised by a school, school district, college, or other educational program. It is important that the question be one that a broad but limited (in time) student work sample can *help* answer. It must be noted, however, that the Slice cannot definitively answer the kinds of questions it typically addresses. It merely provides a text that can provoke useful conversation regarding the questions, one that may lead in turn to new insights.

Details

The Slice Protocol takes anywhere from a morning to nearly a whole day, depending on the amount of student work collected. In our Minnesota example, participants began just after school, paused following the reading to have dinner together, then convened for the seminar after dinner. At

University Neighborhood High School, by contrast, the whole process ran from 9:00 a.m. to noon.

In any case, the Slice Protocol requires a significant amount of preparation. The first task is to settle on a guiding question. The next task is to take steps to ensure the ordinariness and representativeness of the work sample, the slice itself. The power of the protocol ultimately depends on participants' trust that the text they are reading is both ordinary and representative. To ensure these qualities, we encourage the following elements:

- A tight time frame for collection—24 to 36 hours. Teachers and students participating in the selection need to know how to proceed, but they do not need a lot of advance word on the scheduling of the sample. This avoids the temptation to load up the sample with unusual work.
- Randomization in the selection of classes and/or students, though sometimes a stratified random selection makes the most sense. If, for example, a school's guiding question is whether White students and Black students have equal access to a high-quality curriculum, the school will want to ensure equal representation of both groups in the randomized sample. Or if a college's question is whether students are gaining a lot of writing practice regardless of their major, it will want to represent all majors.
- Standardization of the collection procedures. Everyone will or will not collect students' notes. They will or will not include homework. They will or will not take photos. Sometimes a slice-collecting strategy involves a roving photographer who takes photos throughout the school or district, within the same time frame as the collection.

The Minnesota Slice strives only for a reasonable degree of reliability (across collectors) and validity (defined as ordinariness in the collection). The facilitator of the Slice Protocol should always begin by stressing that the readers cannot make valid generalizations from this sample about all of the school's or district's student work. The sample is too limited for this. However, they can use the sample to raise issues for reflection and conversation.

Teachers are often the chief slice collectors. However, in slices that involve older students, we think the students themselves make the better collectors—mostly because they have too many teachers who must otherwise be involved. The trick is to get the student collectors to care about the reliability of the process—either by providing some incentive (University Neighborhood High School offered community service credit), or by offering to debrief them on the process, individually or collectively. Depending on institutional policies, the school or college may have to seek students' and/or parents' permission to include their work in a slice.

Another major preparation effort crucial to the success of the Slice Protocol is the preparation of the text once the collection is over. This involves removing identifying characteristics—especially students' and teachers' names—and coding (to ensure that third-grade work stays with third-grade work and doesn't get mixed in with fifth-grade work). It also involves lots of copying, photo-finishing, and compiling.

Finally, there are details to manage on protocol day: laying out all the photos on a large table or tackboard, or along a corridor wall, or in a continuous projection; arranging the copied work at tables that are themselves arranged in some way—for example, all the freshmen here, all the seniors there, and so on.

The details, in short, are prodigious. In our experience, however, so is the payoff.

Steps

1. *Preparations.* See "Details" above.
2. *Introductions.* The facilitator begins with any introductions that may be appropriate, then identifies the guiding question: "What is the purpose of an education in our town?" "Or how does everyday work at University Neighborhood High School reflect the New York State Learning Standards?" At this point, the facilitator also asks the person in charge of preparations to characterize the slice. How representative is it? What were the parameters for the collection—for example, does it include photos and photocopied notes and jottings? The assumption is that a slice will always be to some extent compromised in its representativeness (and sometimes in its ordinariness, too), and that this is okay as long as the readers are forewarned. (10 minutes or longer, as needed)
3. *Norm-setting.* The facilitator suggests some norms for the reading hour (or even 2 hours for large slices) and asks for assent. These usually include a ban on discussing particular work samples with one another, and indeed a ban on any talking while others are still reading. They may also have to do with such matters as the order in which work is read and the pace and character of the reading (not close but nonetheless thorough), as well as the kind of notes to take (ones related to the guiding question, to patterns of strength and weakness, and so on). (5 minutes including time for clarifying questions as needed)

4. *Reading*. Participants silently read through the entire slice, literally reading the paper-based work and also studying the photos, moving at will among the tables and display areas. (1 hour or more depending on the size of the slice)

5. *Seminar*. Participants discuss the slice in a seminar that follows the reading. The aim of the seminar is to help answer the guiding question, and the facilitator will periodically remind participants that this is the aim. However, it is in the nature of a seminar to follow its own unique conversational paths, and the facilitator will allow this. Useful conversational paths develop best if participants try to build on previous comments and avoid stepping on someone else's talk (that is, starting to speak before the previous speaker has finished). The facilitator welcomes observations and speculations based on evidence in the slice, but discourages sweeping generalizations that are not based on evidence. The facilitator also discourages any participant from providing additional contextual information or explanation—for example, "If we'd only collected the slice the day before, you would have seen a major piece of writing that sixth graders did that day." The facilitator might quickly respond, "Ah, yes, a good reminder that we can't generalize from this slice—just use it to provoke conversation." (45 minutes to an hour)

6. Reflection on the question. Following the seminar, the facilitator asks all participants to reflect briefly in writing on what they have learned from the slice concerning the guiding question. After 5 minutes of writing, the facilitator asks volunteers to share some of what they have written, and invites others to comment. (10 minutes or more depending on the number of participants)

7. *Reflection on the process*. To conclude, the facilitator asks participants to reflect on the protocol itself and what modifications they might suggest, if any. (5 minutes)

Facilitation Tips

The Minnesota Slice puts considerable demands on the facilitator because of its dependence on seminar-based conversation. It helps enormously if the facilitator is practiced in leading text-based discussions. Seminars typically begin when the facilitator asks the first question. It should be an interpretive one—that is, a question that is clearly related to the guiding question and that implicitly prompts references to the text. For example, one seminar in Minnesota began when the facilitator asked, "Will someone get us started by noting some value that you think you see recurring in the work?" A facilitator must prepare for the seminar by constructing at least half a dozen questions like this, and by anticipating possible conversation paths for each (based on his or her own reading of the text). However, most of the questions a good seminar leader asks are not preconstructed, and most of the preconstructed ones are never asked. Among the spontaneous questions are those that probe for evidence ("Can you recall an instance of that in the slice?"); that call for elaboration ("Will you say more?"); and that encourage connections ("Can you relate this idea to what Suzanne said she noticed?").

One crucial role that the facilitator plays is to help the group remember the guiding question: "Let's return for a moment to our guiding question. Remember that we're trying to understand the purpose of education in this town. What purposes did you see below the surface of this work sample?" Another crucial role the facilitator plays is to help the group mind the norms. So, for example, the facilitator interrupts a teacher who is about to explain how a particular piece of work in the slice relates to a larger assignment. "No need to give us more details," the facilitator says. "We all know that the slice provides a very limited window."

Variations

If outsiders are present—as they typically were in Minnesota—the seminar may have the outsiders discuss the slice first—say, for 30 minutes—with the insiders observing. Then the process inverts, giving the insiders the chance to continue the conversation with the outsiders listening, again for 30 minutes. The seminar then finishes with an open conversation to which both groups may contribute.

At University Neighborhood High School, where only faculty were present, and where the guiding question concerned the relationship of the slice to the New York State Learning Standards, the facilitator preceded the reading of the slice with an exercise focused solely on the standards. After reading a two-page summary of the Learning Standards, participants were asked to brainstorm what kinds of work they would expect to see in a high school striving to meet these standards. Later the facilitator began the seminar by asking what the participants had seen of the standards in the slice. After a number of responses and ensuing conversation, he asked what they had missed of the standards in the slice. Following this first alternation of warm and cool responses, the conversation fell naturally into an alternating rhythm, with occasional nudges one way or the other by the facilitator.

Shadow Protocol

Janet Mannheimer Zydney, then a doctoral student at New York University, needed to observe a high school student for a course she was taking, while University Neighborhood High School, fresh from its experience with the Minnesota Slice (see above), wanted to see if slicing could be used to get to know one student more deeply. This is how the Shadow Protocol came to be developed. It aims to see a student's work from the student's own point of view, and involves "shadowing" or accompanying the student through one full day at school.

In the version tried at UNHS, the shadower chronicles the intellectual tasks that the student faces during the day, both within the formal curriculum and also outside it (e.g., in discussions with friends or in extracurricular activities). Assisted by the student, the shadower also collects artifacts concerning the student's response to those tasks. These may include work samples, photos of work in progress, notes of conversation overheard, or quotations from the student's own account of his or her encounter with a task. The shadower aims for low-inference description.

In addition to its relationship to the Minnesota Slice, the Shadow Protocol has roots in "descriptive review" by Pat Carini and the Prospect Center (Featherstone, 1998; Himley, 2000), and in the seminal Collaborative Assessment Conference (see Chapters 1 and 5).

Purpose

The purpose of the Shadow Protocol is to gain a richly contextual perspective on a student's learning—one that helps the teachers understand the student better and teach him or her more effectively.

The Shadow Protocol has four requirements. The first is that the persons who will receive the shadower's report have invited it. They may be the student's teaching team, whose members hope that the report will give them insight into the student's learning. Or they may be a study group that includes only one of the student's teachers, but one who is struggling to understand this particular student and hopes that the report and her colleagues' reflections on it might help. Or they may be the student's Individualized Educational Planning Team, whose members hope to use the report to understand the student's special needs and to make a plan for addressing them. The second requirement is that the student (as well as the student's parents) has consented to the shadowing, understands its purpose, and is prepared to cooperate actively with the shadower. The third requirement is that the shadower—whether an insider (e.g., one of the student's teachers), or an outsider (e.g., a graduate student like Janet)—be both a skillful observer and an experienced low-inference transcriber of observation. (See the variation note below for the School Visit Protocol.) The shadower must also be capable of withholding his or her own interpretations of the findings when presenting the observation data. The protocol depends for its power on the fact that those who commission the data become the principal interpreters of it. Finally, the fourth requirement is that the shadower and the facilitator stay in close communication. Each plays a crucial role in the protocol itself.

Steps

Preparation

1. *Getting acquainted.* The shadower and the student meet to discuss the purpose and format of the shadowing. This meeting is in addition to whatever other preparations have been made—for example, securing parent permission or a conference between the student and a school counselor. The meeting should happen in an informal setting—for example, over breakfast in the school cafeteria the morning before the shadowing, perhaps combined with a brief student-led tour of the school. "So, show me where we'll be going together tomorrow," the shadower might suggest. The shadower emphasizes as they chat or stroll that shadowing is a joint activity—that the shadower will not be able to understand the student's experience unless the student is willing to interpret it for her. The shadower should also answer honestly any questions the student may have—including about the data that result. "I'll be happy to share all my data with you," the shadower might offer, "and I'll also be sharing it with [some of your teachers, or others]. You can help them understand your experience in school just as you'll help me understand it."

2. *Shadowing.* The shadower spends an entire school day with the student, noting the most salient intellectual tasks that the student faces (within and outside the formal curriculum). For each task, the shadower describes the student's response, striving for low-inference description.

3. *Preparation for presentation.* The shadower makes a selection of four to six tasks that seem to represent a variety of responses on the part of the student. The variety may involve levels of interest and engagement, of confidence, of enjoyment, of struggle, or of evident skill and insight. The shadower prepares a brief description of each of the selected tasks and chooses an artifact relating to the student's performances in response to each of the tasks. The artifact might be an assignment completed, quotations from the student's account to the shadower of a hallway conversation with a friend, a photograph of the student's involvement in reading or dancing, or any number of other possible things. These elements are all woven into the shadower's planned presentation.

Protocol

1. *Introduction.* At a conference of the student's teachers or others who invited the shadowing, the facilitator explains the purpose of the protocol: to understand better one student and his or her intellectual strengths by reflecting on a day of his or her life in school. Then the facilitator introduces the shadower. (5 minutes)
2. *Presentation.* The shadower presents a low-inference account of the student's day, as represented in four to six tasks that the student confronted and the work performances that resulted. Often the presentation includes photos that the shadower and student have planned, or samples of the student's work. (20 minutes)
3. *Questions.* The participants ask any questions they may have, and the shadower responds, avoiding in the process anything but minimal inference and interpretation. (10 minutes)
4. *Private speculation.* Based on their reaction to the presentation, participants (including the shadower) individually take time to write down several speculations concerning the student's intellectual strengths. (5 minutes)
5. *Sharing.* Participants (including the shadower) read in turn what they have written, without commentary or questions from others. The shadower should go last. (10–15 minutes)
6. *Open conversation.* Participants discuss the entire set of speculations they have just heard. Prompted by the facilitator, they seek to highlight common threads as well as out-of-the-box insights. Except to answer direct questions in low-inferential ways, the shadower remains silent.
7. *Planning.* Participants brainstorm teaching strategies that build on their new perceptions of the student's strengths. Again, the shadower is silent.
8. *Final word.* The facilitator asks the shadower if he or she has any concluding thoughts based on what he or she has heard in Steps 5 through 7.

Facilitation Tips

It is crucial that the facilitator explain clearly the purpose of this protocol and remind conference participants about this purpose as they offer their speculations. He or she should emphasize that the purpose is to recognize the intellectual strengths of the student so that these can inform teaching. It is not to evaluate the student's curriculum or teachers. Nor is it to evaluate the student's work or work habits. It may be necessary for the facilitator to "ban blame."

Variations

A variation of this protocol might focus on some other observable pattern besides the most salient intellectual tasks and the student's responses to them. For example, the group that commissioned the shadow might like to focus only on the student's opportunities for learning based on social interaction, or on the physical challenges he or she faces in an ordinary day.

Do What You Mean to Do

As we suggested above, the title of this protocol makes a good motto for all the protocols in this chapter, but especially the final four. Both motto and protocol emphasize the crucial role in successful change efforts of clear intentions and follow-through, balanced by attention to feedback. The protocol was developed by Joe McDonald for an NYU Metro Learning Communities facilitative leadership seminar with the leadership staff of New York City's District 79—home of the city's alternative schools. The district leaders were planning a major change and wanted to think together about their plans in a rigorous way. The protocol was inspired by the work of Donald A. Schön, the late MIT philosophy professor whose seminal contributions to education include the concept of the reflective practitioner (Schön, 1983). With Chris Argyris, Schön also advanced the concept of a theory of action (Argyris & Schön, 1996; Schön & McDonald, 1998). Simply put, the idea is that reform efforts in education and elsewhere have distinct but overlapping dimensions of intentionality. First is the intentionality that the reformers consciously espouse (e.g., in their announced purposes). Second is the intentionality wired into their designs (that is, the purposes that seem implicit in the new structures or curricula they build). And third is the intentionality tacitly present in the actions they and others take as they work on reform. Schön argued that these different dimensions of intentionality regularly become misaligned. Reformers may say they mean *this*, but the designs they create may be inadvertently aimed toward some other *that*, as may the actions the reformers take as they work with the designs. To fight such misalignment and help ensure more coherent change efforts overall, Schön argued that reformers should first articulate their intentions as clearly as possible—that is, say what they mean to do and why—even though these formulations are necessarily provisional. He called this "formulating a theory of action," and he offered a handy algebraic way of doing it—urging the reformers to work with their collaborators and evaluators to put flesh on the following skeleton:

In situation S, if you wish to achieve consequence C, do A, given assumptions a^1 through a^n. Here S refers to the particular context, C to the outcome considered desirable, A to the intended action strategy, and a^1 through a^n to the "model of the world" that makes the connection between A and C seem plausible. (Schön & McDonald, 1998, p. 11)

Schön further argued that with the help of evaluators in particular, reformers should continually gather and consider two different kinds of feedback from their theory of action *in* action. The first is single-loop feedback. It assesses the degree of fit with or drift from original intentions, answering the question, How close to the mark are we, how far off? And the second is double-loop feedback, assessing the validity of original assumptions, and answering the question, Is our original intention still best, given our experience to date (Argyris & Schön, 1996; Schön & McDonald, 1998)?

Complete with its algebraic expression, the Do What You Mean to Do protocol may seem the most challenging protocol in this book. Beneath the complex veneer, however, is a tool as simple as its name.

Purpose

The purpose of this protocol is to help change-minded educators construct a theory of action relevant to a project they plan to undertake, or to one they are already engaged in. The thing about a good theory of action, Schön pointed out, is that it is always open to reconsideration.

Details

This protocol is designed for small groups jointly engaged in planning or carrying out a reform or change project of some kind. See "Variations" below for how it might be adapted for groups whose participants are engaged in different reform projects. And see the next protocol, the New Design Protocol, which works well for large groups engaged in a joint project—particularly near the start of planning and when competing intentions may be particularly evident.

Steps

1. *Introduction.* As is often needed with protocols—but particularly this one—the facilitator walks everyone through the steps and/or asks them all to read silently through them. (10 minutes)
2. *Figuring out the theory.* Participants are asked to make sense together of the protocol's introduction (as a whole group or two or three subgroups depending on size). They puzzle in particular over

Schön's algebraic expression, and his and Chris Argyris's idea about feedback. The facilitator encourages them to clarify both what they think they know about "doing what you mean to do" and also what they still need to know about it in order to apply it to their own work. In a visible form (e.g., computer projection or chart paper), a notetaker records the main points of the conversation and the questions it yields. (10 minutes)

3. *Clarifying questions and answers.* The facilitator leads an effort by the whole group to clarify its collective understanding of Schön's and Argyris's ideas. One part of the effort is to answer the questions that the group or groups have raised. The tone of this step should be to reach an adequate understanding, not necessarily an authoritative one. The facilitator might say, "In the end, it doesn't matter if Schön were to pronounce us right or wrong in our interpretation so long as the interpretation is useful to us." The facilitator pronounces the step complete when everyone agrees that they are ready to move on. (5 minutes)

4. *Applying the theory.* In pairs or triads, participants "put flesh" on Schön's algebraic expression. They work with chart paper or a document they can project. (10 minutes)

5. *Presentations.* The pairs or triads present their expressions of their joint project's theory of action. This is done without elaboration, question, or debate. The facilitator says, "Let's just see where the overlaps and conflicts may arise." (5 to 10 minutes depending on the size of the group)

6. *Working toward consensus.* The facilitator leads an effort to develop an expression of the project's theory of action that meets everyone's standard of *adequacy*. In describing this standard, the facilitator reminds the participants that it is in the nature of a theory of action to change over time in response to feedback—particularly double-loop feedback—but that it is important for stakeholders to start off with roughly the same intentions. (10 minutes)

Facilitation Tips

With regard to Step 6, the facilitator should be sensitive to the possibility that actual consensus may take much more time to reach than this or any protocol can allow for. For example, stakeholders who are not present may need to be consulted. Thus the facilitator might aim Step 6 toward provisional consensus, or even just a clear articulation of possible grounds for consensus.

Variations

One variation is to suit a circumstance where protocol participants are planning or involved in different reform activities rather than the same one. In this variation, members of the pairs or triads in Step 4 take turns as presenters and coaches—or, alternatively, depending on available time, one volunteers to present, and the other(s) to coach. Steps 5 and 6 are then replaced by reports from each group on obstacles encountered and progress made, with perhaps reflection by several presenters on what they see as next steps in seeking consensus back home.

Another variation adds a Step 7, where groups consider possible evaluation designs that incorporate ongoing opportunities for single-loop and double-loop feedback. This may be especially helpful in cases where a group reaches consensus early with respect to the theory of action, but has not yet talked with any depth about evaluation, and where an evaluator is present.

New Design Protocol

Vivian Orlen, with help from Alan Dichter, created this protocol to help the faculty of Landmark High School in New York City redesign its accountability system. She originally called it the Building Consensus (Tuning) Protocol. By any name, the protocol is a very useful tool for addressing a common organizational problem that goes something like this: Many if not all people working in the organization think that some kind of major organizational change is needed, but disagree about the specifics. Indeed, factions may have begun to form with regard to these specifics. The protocol gets these rival plans out into the open, renders them discussable, and creates a public search for common ground. In its follow-up steps, a group creates a new design based on the feedback to the ones presented, and the organization then tries to reach consensus with regard to adopting it.

Purpose

The purpose of this protocol is to help reach consensus among teams working to design a solution to a commonly perceived organizational problem.

Details

The protocol is most useful for large groups and in situations where naturally occurring design factions seem evident—that is, distinct groups of people who hold different ideas with respect to the specific nature of the problem or best approach to its solution. The organizational leader (at

Landmark, it was Vivian, who was then the school's principal)—or some otherwise empowered person or group (e.g., a school leadership team)—turns these design factions into officially appointed teams, asking them to put their best thinking forward for all to discuss, with as concrete a set of details as possible. At the same time, this person or group also appoints "synthesizers." These may be a mix of widely trusted insiders and thoughtful outsiders who will listen to the presentations and feedback, stake out the common ground, and assist in the creation of a new design that incorporates the best features of the ones presented.

Teams are asked to develop PowerPoint presentations ahead of time that depict the key details of their designs. They must also prepare "packets"—downloadable background material including their slides—for participants to study prior to the presentations.

Steps

1. *Preparation.* Each team makes its packet available online to all participants at least 24 hours prior to the feedback session. Participants are expected to come to the session familiar with all the designs that will be presented. They are also expected to have highlighted aspects of each that they especially value as well as aspects that they question or dispute for whatever reason.

2. *Presentations.* Each team in turn presents its design. In addition to the design details, the team must present a statement of the problem the design addresses, a rationale for the approach to the problem that it has chosen, its sense of the design's assets and likely impact, and its sense of the design's vulnerabilities. (10 minutes per team)

3. *Clarifying questions.* The purpose of this step—which comes after all the teams have presented—is to enable participants to ask questions they need answered in order to understand any particular design. Examples might include, "Jon's team mentioned 'regular' meetings—specifically, how often would they meet?" or "Lydia's team talked about 'members of the group,' but it wasn't clear to me who the members would be." Examples of questions that are not clarifying questions, but rather *probing* ones, include: "You never mentioned consequences for poor performance. What are you proposing there?" or "How did you decide that this was the best way to proceed?" The facilitator should disallow probing questions by suggesting that participants turn them instead into cool feedback and reserve them for Step 5. (5 minutes)

4. *Warm feedback.* This is the time for all participants to share their sense of the various designs' strengths. This feedback should be specific and should be recorded. The recording helps assure all

participants of the ultimate purpose of the protocol—finding common ground on which to build a new design as well as consensus behind it. This step can either take up each design in turn, or "mix it up" in terms of which design is referred to when. In either case, however, the facilitator should ensure that all the designs get parity of feedback. Participants may not respond to any of the feedback at this point in the protocol, and as usual in adaptations of the Tuning Protocol, the facilitator should remind participants not to mix warm with cool. (10 minutes)

5. *Cool feedback.* Here all participants share any concerns they have with any of the designs, either focused on one design at a time or "mixing it up." As suggested above, cool feedback may be phrased in the form of a probing question. As in Step 4, presenters may not respond at this point, and must not put the cool in warm wrappers. (10 minutes)

6. *Response to feedback.* Speaking in team turns, presenters have a chance to respond to any of the feedback they may choose to respond to. They may not, however, comment here on other teams' designs. (10 minutes)

7. *Synthesizers convene while participants break.* The synthesizers—who may also include the organization's formal leader or leaders—discuss perceived points of emerging consensus, perceived areas of tension, and possible next steps. Everyone else takes a break. (20 minutes)

8. *Synthesizers present their report.* When participants return from break, the synthesizers report their perceptions and suggest next steps. (10 minutes)

9. *Questions and open discussion.* Everyone present gets to ask and answer questions. The facilitator reminds the group that the goal is to build consensus.

10. *New designing.* This is the first of two crucial postprotocol steps. Here, an empowered group—possibly the synthesizers, possibly some delegates from the teams, possibly a leadership group—creates a new design that attempts to incorporate the best and avoid the worst of the presented designs.

11. *Coming to consensus.* The new design is presented, and a new round of warm and cool feedback ensues.

Facilitation Tip

This is a complicated protocol that requires much behind-the-scenes collaborative planning with organizational leaders. It is best facilitated by an outsider who has time and sufficient credibility on the inside to test out leaders' assumptions about the problem and—crucially too—about the emerging design factions. In steps 4 and 5, taking feedback as it comes rather than design by design can highlight common elements across designs.

School Visit Protocol

Alan Dichter created this protocol when he was a Local Instructional Superintendent in New York City, responsible—among other things—for the ongoing professional development of 12 high school principals. He wanted to build a cross-school community to help them solve common problems of practice. He knew that this depended on their gaining a sense of one another's contexts and surmised that this would require interschool visits. Yet "school visits" in New York and elsewhere had become freighted with negative associations. For some, the term suggested the surprise appearance of a supervisor looking for problems to flag on a "walk-through," turning the visit into a kind of compliance audit. For others, the term suggested mandatory or "highly recommended" (by supervisors) tours of "best practice sites"—places where someone "has figured it out already." As the line typically goes, "Visit this place. See what they do. Then do it." Alan knew that visits of this kind can end up making the visitor feel defensive or hopeless about his or her own school. Indeed, both kinds of visits ignore the fact that good schools are always works in progress. None is problem-free. The best are seldom "compliant." And no one has definitively "figured out" solutions to the most important problems in schooling—except provisionally, here and now, for this group or that.

With all this in mind, Alan decided to create a protocol for a kind of visit that acknowledges the nature of school as a continual set of complex challenges that must be managed through steady and thoughtful work informed by good advice. He decided to ask schools to talk with their visitors about their challenges and invite them to offer their advice.

Purpose

The purpose of the School Visit Protocol is to assist colleagues in learning from each other's contexts and the challenges they present. An embedded purpose is to defuse a frequent tendency among educators to be too judgmental of others' practices and too defensive of their own.

Details

An ideal group size is three to five visitors. But bigger groups are possible as long as the school is willing to have them. They will then need to be subdivided into smaller groups for touring purposes. On a school visit the principal participates as chief host, but typically others from the school staff also participate. One of the visitors agrees to participate *and* facilitate. This role needs to be assigned in advance.

Steps

1. *Introductions.* The facilitator opens the visit by asking all participants to introduce themselves. The host principal then gives a brief overview of the school and of some important challenges it is facing. He or she also offers a focus for the visit based on one of these challenges. The focus should be sufficiently narrow to allow the feedback to be specific. The principal might say, for example, "In our high school, we are working on teaching literacy skills across the curriculum. Please look for evidence of this. Also look for opportunities we may be missing."

2. *Preparation for focus.* In order to help them gain the right focus and keep it, the facilitator leads participants through an exercise in imagining findings relevant to the focus—in this case, evidence of and opportunities for literacy teaching across the curriculum. "Given this focus, what might you see or hear?"

3. *Logistics for touring.* The facilitator and host principal then lay out the plan for the touring part of the visit—including the formation of subgroups, the classrooms and other areas to be visited, a suggested length for staying in each place (recommended: at least 15 minutes for a class in session), and any other matters.

4. *Go-round: Evidence.* Following the touring, the participants reassemble. The facilitator begins with a go-round, asking participants to share what they experienced relative to the focus—in this case, evidence of literacy teaching across the curriculum and also of missed opportunities for literacy teaching across the curriculum. At the end of the go-round, the facilitator, who has taken notes, summarizes the feedback.

5. *Go-round: Hypothesis.* In a second go-round participants explain why they think they found what they found. In effect, they offer a hypothesis of where the school stands in relation to the challenge it has set for itself. Again, the facilitator ends the round with a summary.

6. *Go-round: Advice.* Based on the evidence—present and missing—as well as hypotheses to account for the evidence, the participants offer advice in a third go-round. The advice might involve ideas about

how to test the hypotheses, or how to collect further evidence. One can think of Steps 4, 5, and 6 as What? So What? Now What? (See the protocol of the same name at www.schoolreforminitiative.org.) A recent adaptation of What? So What? Now What?—one that puts an emphasis on data—follows next in this chapter.

7. *Host's response.* The host principal is offered a chance to comment on anything that he or she has heard. If time permits, a brief open discussion may follow.

8. *Debriefing.* In a fourth go-round, participants each say what they have learned from the visit.

Facilitation Tips

Visitors naturally bring interests of their own to a school visit—ones that may color what they see and report. The facilitator might acknowledge this at the end and ask participants to share any special interests during the debriefing round. However, the facilitator should also be alert earlier to any signs that visitors' interests may be interfering with the host's focus—and should call participants on this. The facilitator should also bring a special sensitivity to Step 6. Here, giving advice is not license to impose one's own vision or theory of action. It must address the school's focus and be grounded in the evidence and hypotheses that emerged in the earlier steps.

Variation

Joe McDonald uses a variation of this protocol in which the visitors are not principals but student teachers from other schools. The focus of the visits is the students' challenges, not the schools'—for example, learning how to teach English language learners or to establish classroom routines. And the steps are different too: raising questions, making low-level inferences (grounded in observations of teachers and students), and offering insights gained about their own learning relative to the focus of the visit.

For another variation, see the school-visit protocol associated with the work of the Instructional Rounds group at Harvard (City, Elmore, Fiarman, & Teitel, 2009).

What Do We Know? What Do We Suspect? What Do We Need to Find Out?

This protocol is one of two complementary data-focused protocols in this new edition of the book. The other is in Chapter 6 and is called the

Looking at Data Protocol. It assists in the close reading and interpretation of a single data set. This one, by contrast, takes a broader view—beginning with an inventory about what is already known (about a particular topic) and proceeding through a planning stage for further inquiry.

The protocol is a derivative of another protocol called What? So What? Now What? It was a favorite of Nancy Mohr's. She and many other leaders and facilitators have used What? So What? Now What? to help change-oriented teams focus on high-leverage issues, set smart goals, and plan effective action steps (see www.schoolreforminitiative.org/doc/what_so_what.pdf). After years of using it himself, however, Alan Dichter came to think that What? So What? Now What? tends to generate unwarranted assumptions in the first two steps and thus faulty action plans in the third. His replacement questions in this new protocol are meant to lend more empirical weight to the moment when plans first gel. Thus the protocol starts with attention to data: What do we know—based on specific available data? It then licenses data-based speculation: What do we suspect, given some data points or data patterns? Finally, it proposes data-generating action steps: What do we need to find out? In contrast to the original protocol, Alan's derived protocol slows down reform action, but in exchange for better direction.

Purpose

This protocol is meant to ground reform action in data-focused conversation and planning. Typically, it is used with participants who are familiar with the context and likely to be themselves affected by the change effort. However, the protocol works well too as a device for unpacking a complex case with which participants are not already familiar—as, for example, in a graduate course on change-oriented leadership.

Details

Participants work through the steps of the protocol in groups of 5 to 10, with multiple groups possible (particularly in online adaptations). The data involved may be quantitative, qualitative, or preferably both—for example, test scores and student work samples. In any case, it helps if the facilitator or some other member of the group is familiar with the properties of the data and able to orient others to the data set(s).

In the version we present below, the protocol is blended. That is, it begins online (with the downloading of data) but then unfolds face to face. (See McDonald et al., 2012, for the wholly online version.)

Steps

1. *Preparation.* In collaboration with leaders of the change effort, the facilitator selects relevant data sets, and makes them available for participants to download—typically with information about the sources and properties of the data, and some advice for how to interpret them. Generally, the facilitator also frames the next step. For example, he or she might say, "As you know, the change effort [we're engaged in or studying] is focused on achievement in mathematics, and the data we've assembled are relevant to this focus. In the next 24 hours [or whatever duration makes sense given the complexity of the data] read the data and jot down four or five things that you think are evident in them. Nothing is too small or too 'obvious' to notice and record."

2. *What do we know?* The facilitator might begin by asking pairs to share their lists of jottings with each other. This may help alleviate any misunderstandings about the data or misinterpretations of them. Then participants each share one thing that they think seems evident in the data. The rounds of sharing might be repeated two or three times in order to gain some analytical breadth. The facilitator or a designated recorder keeps track of what all the participants think they "know." In the process the facilitator may need to caution against sweeping interpretations. For example, he or she might say, "Whoa, I'm not sure we *know* that yet, but we might *suspect* it, so save this for the next step of the protocol." At the end of the step the facilitator should invite others also to challenge elements on the overall list of "knowns." To ensure that this invitation is safe for all, the facilitator should add that in this protocol, whatever item makes it to a list is open to anyone's challenge or revision, and that the person who first suggested the item should resist the urge to "defend" it.

3. *What do we suspect?* As in Step 1, participants share in turn one thing they "suspect" based on the data, perhaps beginning with some challenged items from the list of "knowns." The facilitator urges them to stay on focus and to remain data-based, but also to take risks. For example, he or she might say, "Remember that this is headed toward helping us figure out what else we need to know about the state of mathematics teaching in the school, and don't worry about raising suspicions that might not pan out. We won't take action until we know more." Again, as in Step 2, a list of suspicions emerges here, and the facilitator ends the step by asking for any comments about any items on this list.

4. *What do we need to find out?* In this step participants share one thing (per round, with multiple rounds possible) that they think would be valuable to find out more about in order to confirm, inform, or refute a particular "suspicion." The step begins, however, with an invitation by the facilitator to study the list of suspicions. And it ends with yet another list, though one that has now been honed by quite a bit of focused thinking.
5. *Final step.* Various final steps are possible depending on the context. Graduate students of change-oriented leadership might simply discuss what they have learned from this case. Colleagues preparing for change might discuss which of the inquiries listed on the Step 4 list they want to commit to undertaking and how.

CHAPTER 5

Working with Texts

RESPONSIBLE DIRECTION OF our own education as professional educators necessarily involves consulting with many others by means of the texts they produce. These others may be experts in the subjects we teach, in the development of learners (including us), in the dynamics of organizations, in the theories and policies that undergird our work, and much more. They may even be our own colleagues and students. The texts they create may take the form of statistical tables, verbal narratives and descriptions, photographs, videos, audios, or multimedia compositions. We may access them in person, in print, or online. Whatever the form or means of access, however, our ability to make sense of the wisdom and provocations of others as captured in texts is central to our continuing professional development.

Among the questions we take up in this chapter are the following: How do we best dig into texts to extract what we need? How can we read them collaboratively—in ways that harness the power of multiple perspectives? How do we apply our best reading skills—in terms of decoding, inference, interpretation, and critique—to data texts, nonverbal texts, and multimedia texts? Finally, how do we make certain that the expertise we call on by various means meshes appropriately with our interests and needs?

Collaborative Assessment Conference

Roughly once a month on a Saturday throughout the academic year, Steve Seidel convenes a group of as many as 30 educators in a large conference room on the campus of Harvard University. Called "Rounds," the meetings attract some longtime devotees. After a quick breakfast of coffee and bagels, the educators take their seats in a large circle surrounded by portraits of past deans of the Harvard Graduate School of Education. Then one of them presents some student work that he or she has brought. Thus commences a Collaborative Assessment Conference—the home-office version of ones that happen now in many other places, thanks to the wide influence of Harvard Project Zero and to the availability of two rich descriptions of the protocol, one by Seidel (1988) himself, and another by Tina Blythe, David Allen, and Barbara Powell (1999/2007).

Purpose

This protocol has several purposes, according to Seidel. The first is to enhance teachers' perceptions of all their students' work by honing the teachers' perceptual skills. A second is to encourage depth of perception by demonstrating all that can be seen in a single student's work. A third is to encourage a balance in perception—the habit of looking for strength as well as need. The assumption behind this purpose is that a teacher can address need only by building on strength. A fourth purpose is to encourage conversation among teachers about what the work shows and how they can act individually and collectively on what it shows in order to benefit their students.

Unlike many protocols for looking at student work, the Collaborative Assessment Conference typically focuses attention on one student's work at a time. This is because of its interest in honing perception and its assumption that care in attending to one student can generalize to care in attending to many.

Also unlike many other protocols, this one does not pay overt attention to a set of learning standards. Still, it involves standards—implicitly, but purposefully. This is because the honing of perception is ultimately and effectively the honing of standards, too, and conversation about students' work inevitably involves "tuning" standards, even when the word *standards* never comes up (McDonald, 2001).

Details

Time varies from 45 to 90 minutes. The variance is a function of the number of participants, the number of student work samples considered, and to some extent, the facilitator's discretion in terms of the timing of steps. A group setting is required in which participants (5–30) have access to the work under study and where eye contact can be maintained as much as possible. Although the protocol can work well with a single piece of work, as long as it is rich in detail, presenters are ordinarily asked to provide several pieces of work by the same student, as, for example, in a portfolio. Typically, participants all have copies of the work presented when it involves writing or drawing. Other media can be posted or displayed so that everyone can view it at once. To get a good sense of the kind of work that might be presented at a Collaborative Assessment Conference, see the archive of student work co-curated by Seidel and connoisseur of student work Ron Berger at the website of Expeditionary Learning Schools, where Berger is Chief Program Officer (elschools.org/student-work).

Steps

1. *Presenting.* The facilitator begins the Conference by asking the presenting teacher what he or she has brought for the group to examine. The teacher then presents a single student's work, offering only minimal context. He or she might merely say, for example, that this is the work of a third-grade boy. Participants read silently or otherwise examine the work, noting any features that hold particular significance for them.

2. *Describing.* The facilitator asks the group, "What do you see?" Group members respond by describing components or aspects of the work without making judgments of quality.

3. *Raising questions.* The facilitator asks, "What questions does this work raise for you?" Participants respond with questions they have about the student, the work, the assignment, the classroom circumstance, and so forth. During this time, the presenting teacher listens and makes notes, but does not respond.

4. *Speculating.* The facilitator asks, "What do you think this student is working on?" Responders say what they think the student was attempting to learn, accomplish, practice, or improve. The facilitator presses for evidence to support these speculations: "Why do you think this student is working on . . . ?"

5. *Responding.* The facilitator invites the presenting teacher to speak: "After hearing all this, what are your thoughts?" This is the presenter's chance to respond to questions raised, to offer additional context, to share his or her own thoughts about the student work, and to respond to any other questions participants may have regarding the student, the context, the assignment, and so forth. At this time the presenter might also share any surprises or unexpected feedback heard during the earlier steps.

6. *Reflecting and discussing.* The facilitator invites open discussion, asking participants to reflect on the experience of the protocol by the light of their own larger experiences in teaching and learning. He or she may also ask participants to share what they found particularly helpful or difficult while participating in the activity, and also how they might use the protocol in their own work with colleagues and/ or students.

Facilitation Tips

More so than in most other protocols, the facilitator here plays the interlocutor, initiating each of the steps with a particular question. Moreover, he or she may use questions to ensure protocol discipline. For example, if a participant responds to the question "What do you see in this work?" with an evaluative comment, the facilitator might ask, "What elements do you see that made you think so?" He or she might also simply ask the participant to withhold evaluative comments.

Like all protocols, this has a number of features that strike participants as unnatural the first time through. Here it seems unnatural to know so little context to start. The facilitator may have to prevent the presenter from providing too much and thus distorting the seeing and responding. Similarly, the facilitator may have to encourage the participants to raise questions about the work rather than just about the context.

A major objective of the facilitator here—especially when working with an inexperienced group—is to press participants to go deeply into the work, to raise more questions and make more speculations collectively than any one member imagined possible. Another objective is to generate questions and speculations that cause participants to think more deeply about learning and teaching. In this regard, the facilitator may on occasion have to guard against superficiality. For example, sometimes an inexperienced group will respond to the question, "What do you think the student is working on?" by answering simply, "a math problem" or "an art assignment," and the facilitator must point out that the purpose of the question is not to guess the assignment, but to speculate about how the student frames the learning involved. The excitement of a Collaborative Assessment Conference derives from how much can be learned from a single student's creative work.

Unlike some protocols described in this book, the Collaborative Assessment Conference has no preset time limits assigned for each step. This means that the facilitator must gauge the overall time well—since overall time is always limited—and must also attend closely at each step to signs that the group may be ready to move on to the next step. This is tricky, because this protocol may also demand more than an ordinary amount of "wait time"— for example, to encourage as many questions and speculations as possible. The facilitator should listen for comments that may be more appropriate to a later step. Hearing one, the facilitator should ask the person to restate the comment at the appropriate time. Hearing several, however, may be a signal that people are ready to move on.

Variations

If the group includes some experienced facilitators, they can facilitate smaller groups, thus enabling several simultaneous conferences to occur. For a large group, a useful variation is to "fishbowl" the conference: A group of 6 to 10 volunteers, with an experienced facilitator and a predesignated presenter, participates in the review while others observe. Step 6 should then be open to the observers as well as the participants.

Final Word

This is a very versatile protocol developed by Daniel Baron and Patricia Averette for the National School Reform Faculty. It is useful in exploring any kind of text, including controversial ones. For example, in a graduate preservice teacher education course, Beth McDonald uses it to explore some texts concerning racial identity—a crucial topic in the course, but a risky one too. Neither the texts that Beth uses nor the topic itself lend themselves easily to open discussion. When texts or topics are especially challenging, open discussions can easily fail, as some students dominate, others retreat into silence, and important viewpoints stay unexpressed..

Students come to Beth's class having read Peggy McIntosh's (1989) essay "White Privilege: Unpacking the Invisible Knapsack," and also Beverly Tatum's (1992) powerful piece about racial identity. Beth then arranges the class into groups of three students each and follows the steps outlined below, managing the time herself by calling out the switches, rather than relying on the group's own timekeeping. She tells her students that the timing will be "rigid for a purpose," but that they will have more relaxed time later to talk about whatever the timing may squeeze out. The version presented here is one developed and favored by Beth.

Purpose

The purpose of the Final Word Protocol is to expand the interpretation of one or more texts by encouraging the emergence of a variety of interests, viewpoints, and voices. By forcing everyone to offer an interpretation, and to listen closely to and reflect back others' interpretations, Final Word ensures the emergence of diverse perspectives on texts. It also helps participants feel safer in proposing what may be offbeat or dissident interpretations because the protocol implicitly avoids consensus building. It is okay in this protocol to end a session with as much difference of interpretation in the air as was there at the start. The point is to get it into the air.

Details

Final Word generally takes from 30 to 60 minutes (depending on group size) and is best done in groups of 3 to 6. It works especially well when the facilitator wants a large group to engage with the same text and breaks it into smaller groups. Participants must have copies of the text(s). Texts may have been read in advance, or they may be read on the spot (although then they must be short, and the facilitator must allow for varied reading times and for a bit of mulling over). A countdown timer can be a very helpful tool for this and other protocols with tight timelines.

Steps

1. *Introduction and selection.* The facilitator introduces the whole protocol, providing copies of a short list of the steps involved. Then he or she asks all participants to select from one of the texts a short passage that has particular meaning for them, a meaning they would like to call attention to.
2. *Arrangement.* The whole group breaks into tight circles of three to six participants each. The facilitator assigns an order of presentation for participants in each circle—for example, "The person in your group whose back is most turned to the door is number one, and the person to his or her right is number two, and so on." Each circle is asked to assign a strict timekeeper within each group. Alternatively, the facilitator can serve as timekeeper for the entire room, calling out the time switches.
3. *Presentation.* Presenter number one presents the passage he or she has identified, reading aloud and having people follow along on their copies. The presenter speaks for 2 or 3 uninterrupted minutes about it (with the timing clear in advance).
4. *Reflecting back.* Each listener in turn has 1 uninterrupted minute to "reflect back" on what the presenter has said. The facilitator has explained that reflecting back means exploring the presenter's interpretation of the passage, not adding one's own interpretation. A listener might begin, "From what you said, I can see that you are concerned about . . ."
5. *Final word.* The round ends with a 1-minute uninterrupted time for the presenter to react to what has just been said.
6. *Round repeats.* Rounds two, three, and so on follow until all members of each group have presented and have had their final word.
7. *Written reflection.* Following the rounds, the facilitator asks everyone to write for 5 minutes about what they have learned from the rounds about the text(s) as a whole. This might be followed by a go-round asking each member to share one observation or insight. In a group with some history and trust, the facilitator might ask volunteers to share something they heard from someone else that they found surprising, moving, or otherwise provocative.

Facilitation Tips

When the facilitator keeps the time, he or she risks feeling like an intrusive announcer ("May I have your attention, please? Time to switch presenters!") or the caller in a square dance ("Readyyy? SWITCH presenters!"). However, when the groups do their own timing, there is the probability that they will finish at different times. There is also a significant risk that they will succumb to the temptation to dispense with artificiality. But without the artifice, Final Word becomes a small-group discussion, which is a different learning vehicle.

Groups may be bigger than three, and bigger groups raise more viewpoints and more possibility of hearing diverse interpretations. But, of course, the process takes longer, with more rounds as well as more time per round.

Facilitators should take particular care with Step 4. This is where presenters can experience really being heard—a crucial (and often unusual) experience for many. It helps in describing Step 4 to say, "It's not what you think about the presenter's passage. It's what you think you heard the *presenter* say (and think and feel) about the passage." There are some variations of Final Word, however, that change the emphasis of Step 4. See "Variations" below.

Some facilitators—particularly when they are teachers who feel accountable for students' understanding of the text(s)—find it disconcerting that they cannot hear what all the conversations touch upon. We suggest they get over that, and give accountability a broader scope.

Variations

Sometimes Final Word facilitators ask speakers in Step 4 to provide their own reactions to the text passage, rather than reflect on the presenter's. This has the advantage of getting more interpretations into the open, but the disadvantage of not attending fully to any one interpretation. However, there may be times when this makes sense. A protocol called Save the Last Word for Me takes this variation further and offers still other benefits. In Save the Last Word each presenter merely reads the passage or passages selected, withholding any comment until the listeners have first had their turns to comment. Then the presenter's "last word" incorporates not only his or her original interest in the passage but also what he or she has learned about it from the other members of the circle. This variation is useful in encouraging presenters to pick particularly complex or ambiguous passages—perhaps ones that they think are important, but do not feel they fully understand. It has the added advantage of increasing the likelihood that the conversation will remain more "text-based" with no initial interpretation to respond to. (See the face-to-face version of Save the Last Word for Me at www.schoolreforminitiative.org/doc/save_last_word.pdf, or an online version in McDonald et al., 2012).

Jigsaw Protocol

It is worth noting that Elliot Aronson and Shelley Patnoe (1997) devised the Jigsaw strategy of cooperative learning for the Austin Public Schools to help educators there deal with conflicts associated with racial desegregation. The purpose was to create structures that bring students together for learning and dialogue across racial lines and in the process enable them to get to know one another as people. In devising a protocol based on their work, Beth McDonald was mindful of its association with equity as well as with texts.

Jigsawing in general involves using two stages of small-group work. In the first—or expert group stage—small groups study different facets of a topic. For example, one group might examine and discuss materials related to the habitat of a particular animal, while another group examines and discusses material related to the reproductive system of the animal, and so on. In the second stage, the experts move into jigsaw groups, each composed of at least one member from each expert group. Here the purpose is to share expertise—and assemble a fuller understanding of the animal or other topic. In her teaching, Beth McDonald frequently creates and implements versions of Jigsaw as a means of having students take responsibility for sharing what they've learned from texts (or parts of texts) that not all students have been assigned. The following version was used for the first time when students had read different chapters from the same book, and Beth was looking for a fresh discussion structure.

Purpose

This protocol can be used to allow participants access to learning from a greater amount of text than time would permit had everyone read or viewed the same texts.

Details

The Jigsaw protocol can be undertaken with any size group. The facilitator provides sufficient copies of the texts to be read by the various groups, or pre-assigns them—for example, via web links (see "Variations"). They may be parts of the same whole—for example, chapters from the same book— or separately authored texts that relate to the same topic. They can be verbal, visual, or multimedia texts.

Steps

1. *Introduction and grouping.* The facilitator introduces the activity and arranges participants into groups of three to five. The groups can be randomized by counting off. Texts are assigned to each group. (5 minutes)
2. *Reading and individual highlighting.* Participants read their group's text individually, and highlight key points from their own perspective. Reading time will vary with the length and difficulty of the texts assigned. For less experienced readers, the teacher might demonstrate highlighting—for example, with a read-aloud/think-aloud and comments on a projected text.
3. *Discussion and group highlighting.* In each of these small groups, participants share and discuss what they feel to be the key points from the reading. After discussion, they coconstruct and record a list of key points for sharing in the jigsaw groups. (20 minutes)
4. *Jigsaw group sharing.* The groups are reconfigured so that each jigsaw group has at least one expert prepared to teach others about his or her group's text. Group members take turns sharing the collection of key points with the others. The facilitator may decide that a certain order of sharing makes sense based on the topic—for example, starting with habitat and ending with reproduction. Clarifying questions and discussion can occur throughout this step. (40–60 minutes, depending on group size)
5. *Individual writing.* Individually, participants make notes capturing their learning from the jigsaw session.
6. *Go-round.* As time permits, the facilitator invites some or all participants to share one idea from the session that holds particular significance for them. (10 minutes)
7. *Debriefing.* The facilitator invites participants to comment on the process. (5 minutes)

Variations

The protocol can be used to view and share a selection of films, or web pages, or to share reactions to visits involving several classrooms or community sites. For films or other long texts, Steps 1 and 2 are done before the meeting or the class.

A variation that Beth McDonald has used substitutes a "gallery walk" for the jigsaw step (Step 4). The expert group members record key points on large chart paper and post them for all to see. Participants visit each chart and add questions or comments to them using Post-it notes. After the gallery walk, the experts reconvene at the chart they made and respond orally to some of the comments.

Panel Protocol

Alan Dichter once found himself planning a retreat for principals to which a panel of experts had already been invited. Alan's problem was what to do with the experts. The usual "everybody talks for 10 minutes [which typically becomes 20], then we'll have the discussant discuss, and finally open the floor to questions [when there's little time left for any]" seemed a horrible way to spend precious retreat time. So Alan designed an alternative.

He asked each expert to write a one-page case study based on a problem that he or she thought a group of principals ought to wrestle with. Small groups of principals worked on the case studies, trying to solve the problems, while the experts observed their work. Following the activity, the experts were finally impaneled—but now their audience was primed to hear what they had to say about the problems they had brought.

Purposes

The main use of the Panel Protocol is to make sure that a group of educators gets to interact meaningfully with some outsiders whose expertise it needs, instead of being bored by "talking heads." At the same time, the protocol's additional purpose is to help the experts think about and frame their expertise so that it best meets the needs of the people they are trying to help. All too often, experts are hastily briefed and arrive with too limited a perspective on how they might best contribute.

Details

The protocol generally takes about 2 hours. The size of the overall group can vary substantially, as can the size of the small work groups. The panel can similarly come in many sizes, although three to four panelists seems ideal. If the room is very large, a wireless microphone is helpful.

The experts are each asked to prepare for the panel by developing a written case study focused on a problem of professional practice. They may substitute, if they choose, one developed by someone else. The cases should be more or less complex depending on the time that will be available for wrestling with them. A one-page case for a 2-hour protocol is appropriate. The cases should be written in a way that highlights the ambiguities and uncertainties of professional practice, and should end with questions to prompt readers to identify next steps. The following, for example, are good closing questions:

- In light of the information you have, what action would you take?
- Was there any action that should have been taken earlier but was not?
- What additional information do you need to act?
- How would you proceed to get that information?

Steps

1. *Introduction.* The facilitator explains the steps to follow, and asks the experts to introduce themselves and give a brief description of their area(s) of expertise.
2. *Case reading.* Small groups each receive one prewritten case, with each case going to at least two groups. The facilitator allows ample reading time and encourages notetaking.
3. *Case interpretation.* For a 2- to 3-hour protocol, groups get 20–30 minutes to work on interpreting the case and trying to solve the problem it highlights. During this time, they also prepare a 2- or 3-minute presentation. This presentation should include an answer to the question, "What is this a case of?"—an answer that will help participants who did not read the case to understand the rest of the presentation. The presentation should also include a short list of action steps and an acknowledgment of either the group's consensus or not regarding them.
4. *Expert consultation.* During work time, groups may call over the experts to answer specific questions. But the facilitator has coached the experts to avoid giving elaborate responses to these questions and to avoid providing overall "solutions" to the case problems. When they are not engaged in answering "call-overs," the experts wander the room and listen in.
5. *Presentations.* Following the small-group work time, the facilitator announces the first case, calling on all the groups who worked on it to make their presentations in turn. Following all the presentations on a particular case, the facilitator invites all participants to react or ask questions. Presentations of additional cases continue in this fashion until all the cases have been presented and discussed. (5–15 minutes per case)
6. *Expert panel reactions.* After a break, the experts assemble into a panel to react to what they have heard. The facilitator suggests that they focus especially on the strengths and weaknesses of the various action

steps proposed for the case they wrote, and that they take the opportunity as well to point out what they think the groups may have overlooked. The facilitator has privately suggested to them that this format offers them an opportunity to reinforce principles they think should guide decision making in practice. Each expert, in turn, gets a maximum of 10 to 15 minutes of reaction time.

7. *Questions and comments.* Participants react to the experts' perspectives.

Facilitation Tips

The facilitator must meet with the experts beforehand. It is crucial that they understand their role and how it departs from the ordinary. They may need assurance that they will have plenty of time in Step 6 to share their expertise, and that the participants, having wrestled with the cases they wrote, will be far more receptive to learning from this expertise than they would be if they had walked cold into a conventional panel-of-experts presentation. The experts should be encouraged to use Step 4 as an opportunity to discern what the participants already seem to know and also what they still need to know.

If the group is very large, it may not be possible for all the teams to report out. Instead, the facilitator may ask one team to report, and give a few minutes at the end for other teams working on the same case to offer another viewpoint or "crucial action step" if one comes to mind.

In handling the final question-and-answer portion (Step 7), the facilitator may encourage the experts to take 5 to 10 questions before answering any of them. Not only does this allow the experts a chance to synthesize their responses, often focusing on themes and reinforcing broader issues, but it decreases the likelihood that the panel as a whole will get stuck on one point.

Variation

Joe McDonald and his colleagues use the Panel Protocol at NYU to introduce students in the teacher education and counseling programs to the idea of a "caring professional." The experts typically include a youth worker, a social worker, a drug counselor, and a principal. The cases are brief and ambiguous accounts—all drawn from the panelists' experience—of violence or suspected violence in children's lives: bullying, child abuse, self-destructive behavior, and so on. The small groups post their insights and questions with regard to the cases on chart paper rather than report them out verbally, and everyone—including the panelists—walks around the room to check them out during the break, gaining in the process more opportunity to think about how to respond to them.

Mars/Venus Protocol

Inspiration for the name of this protocol, which deals with all kinds of contrasting viewpoints, comes from John Gray's (1992) book about gender differences in communication. Beth McDonald created the protocol for a class session of a course for which half the students had read Alfie Kohn's *The Schools Our Children Deserve* (2000) and the other half E. D. Hirsch's *The Schools We Need* (1999). The goal of the session was to promote analysis and deeper understanding of one's own text while gaining some understanding of the other.

Purpose

This protocol is useful in helping people learn from contrasting points of view, particularly when one of the views is less familiar. It works especially well when a group has been split into two reading groups in order to tackle two contrasting texts.

Details

The protocol runs anywhere from 1 hour to 90 minutes and may involve any number of participants, divided into subgroups of four participants each (homogeneously composed with respect to the text read). The facilitator should preselect and reproduce four or five substantial quotations from each of the contrasting texts for use by the subgroups.

Steps

1. *Introduction.* The facilitator explains that the purpose of the exercise is to further explore and understand the text each participant has read through exposure to a contrasting point of view. To start, group members are given the set of quotations from the "other" text, that is, the one they have not read. The facilitator prompts the groups as follows: "Based on your reading of him, how do you think E. D. Hirsch (or Alfie Kohn) would respond to each of these statements by Alfie Kohn (or E. D. Hirsch)? Would the two agree or disagree? What underlying beliefs of your author does each quotation either tap or challenge?" (5 minutes)
2. *Reading.* The participant allows sufficient time for each group member to read the quotations individually and to think about them privately in the light of their previous reading. (10–15 minutes)

3. *Facilitation and discussion.* Group members take turns facilitating as they discuss each quotation, sharing their responses to the prompt. (25–30 minutes)
4. *Summarizing.* Each subgroup prepares a brief summary to share with the whole group regarding what it has discovered concerning the authors' differences and similarities of perspective. (5–10 minutes)
5. *Open conversation.* The facilitator opens the floor to the groups, asking each group to report the highlights of its summary, and invites others to share reactions or clarifying questions. (15 minutes)
6. *Reflection.* The facilitator asks the large group to reflect on the value and challenges of the activity. (5–10 minutes)

Facilitation Tips

To avoid the potential for a superficial and dismissive treatment of the opposing text, it is important that the facilitator highlight the need to look for the underlying bases for any disagreements, along with potential areas of agreement. When this works well, participants will have a more complex understanding of the issues that are under consideration.

Variation

Groups can be asked to make a chart-paper summary for posting during the summarizing step. Then, instead of oral reporting, the whole group can engage in a "gallery walk" to read other summaries before the open conversation step.

Text Rendering Protocol (Video Version)

The Text Rendering Protocol is widely used by educators affiliated with the School Reform Initiative, an organization that maintains an extensive online collection of protocols and also hosts an annual Winter Meeting where novices and experienced facilitators alike practice using the collection (see www.schoolreforminitiative.org and www.schoolreforminitiative.org/doc/text_rendering.pdf). The original version of the Text Rendering Protocol asks participants to read a print-based text and, as they read, to select passages that seem to them particularly useful in exploring a topic of interest to the whole group. The selection is highly constrained: one sentence from anywhere in the text, one phrase (again from anywhere), and one word. Working in successive go-rounds, participants then share their sentences, phrases, and words, and explain their choices with references to the topic of interest. In the process, they experience a rather thorough discussion of the topic, but one with unusually divergent perspectives and strong textual moorings. Often facilitators have the participants write their phrases and then their words on sentence strips to post, or in a projected Googledoc. The result is often poetic.

In this adaptation of the protocol, the text is a video—in the example offered here, a video of teaching. Joe McDonald made the adaptation with the resources of the Teaching Channel in mind—a large and diverse online collection of teaching videos (see www.teachingchannel.org).

Purpose

The ultimate purpose of the Text Rendering Protocol is to enlarge a group's understanding of a topic of common interest. The protocol begins by surfacing what viewers take note of while viewing a video with the common interest in mind. For example, a group of teachers or teacher education students may use a particular video downloaded from the Teaching Channel to explore a complex teaching practice like orchestrating a discussion or to gain insight into teaching to the Common Core Standards or working with English language learners.

Details

In this variation, the typical text-rendering focus on sentence, phrase, and word becomes a focus instead on motif (or recurring element), scene, and image—though with the order reversed. Images are most readily discerned, while scenes are apparent only when they shift, and motifs only when reflected upon.

The time required for this protocol varies depending on the number of participants, and whether one or more videos are viewed and discussed. Or participants may each have brought a short video from their own teaching—each requiring a text rendering.

The means of viewing the videos may also vary, especially depending on the number of participants—from a large-screen video projection to laptops or tablet computers in face-to-face versions. The protocol also lends itself well to online work—whereby each participant views the video(s) in his or her own time and space, and comments in a series of online postings and reactions. The Teaching Channel website has a handy built-in annotation tool also, so noting points where images, scenes, or motifs occur or recur is relatively easy.

Steps

1. *Introduction.* The facilitator reviews the steps of the protocol, and establishes a clear focus for viewing and noting in terms of a topic of interest. Then he or she asks the participants to make note of images of interest (with regard to the topic), scenes of interest, and motifs of interest. It helps to define an *image* as something that can be captured by a pause button; a *scene* as something that falls between cuts or shifts of the camera's focus; and a *motif* as any image (whether visual, aural, or both) that recurs.

2. *Viewing and noting.* Viewers watch with the topic of interest in mind, and note images, scenes, and motifs of interest—literally *note* (e.g., on paper, Post-its, a Google doc, or by using an annotation tool if available).

3. *Go-round: Image.* Each participant selects one image to discuss, and explains briefly its relevance to the topic of interest. (1 minute per participant)

4. *Go-round: Scene.* Each participant selects one scene to discuss, and explains briefly its relevance to the topic of interest. (1 minute per participant)

5. *Go-round: Motif.* Each participant selects one motif to discuss, and explains briefly its relevance to the topic of interest. (1 minute per participant)

6. *Open discussion.* The facilitator asks participants to discuss what they have learned about the topic of interest as a result of the focus on images, scenes, and motifs. (10 minutes or more)

Facilitation Tips

Some viewers may have difficulty discerning motifs within a video, either because the video lacks them or because the viewers lack sufficient reflection time. Facilitators should allow a pass on this round as needed. Similarly, short videos may not lend themselves to analysis by scene. The protocol can easily proceed instead in multiple rounds focused exclusively on images. This may work especially well if multiple short videos are viewed.

The facilitator should begin the open-discussion step by asking participants to look at all the elements that have been noted and recorded and try to keep their discussion comments grounded in these.

Variation

Another good way to discuss a video by the light of a common topic of interest is to use the Save the Last Word for Me protocol rather than the

Text Rendering Protocol as the discussion vehicle (see "Variations" under Final Word above). Thus each participant describes an image, scene, or motif as a discussion topic for the other participants and ends the round with his or her own discussion of it. For example, the participant might begin his or her round by saying, "I would like us to focus on how Ms. Barnes uses the whiteboard—what she chooses to write on it and when. How does this figure in the discussion she is managing?"

Art Feedback Protocols

At Millennium High School in New York City, teachers were trained in the use of protocols for their own professional development. But many quickly imagined using protocols in teaching too, and some became protocol designers. One is Jennifer Krumpus who created the Art Feedback Protocols below. "When I first started teaching art," she explained, "I was amazed by the ability students had to take conceptual risks and experiment with materials, but I was equally appalled at their inability to articulate this process and reflect on it. I quickly recognized that there was a whole other component of art education I had to engage in." She began by developing scaffolds for peer review that she called scripts—comparing them to the lines that actors initially read, then later internalize and use with genuine feeling and expression. She knew, from experience, that providing models of conversations or what she called "scripts" could help her students eventually participate productively in more open-ended ways.

Purpose

The purpose of the Art Feedback Protocols (Getting Suggestions and What Do You See) is to help novice artists meet two challenges with respect to giving and receiving peer feedback. The first involves giving feedback specific enough to be useful. And the second has to do with understanding that an artist's intentionality is not the sum of a work's meaning—that the work can be quite successful even when the observer takes away something completely different from what the artist intended.

Jennifer introduces these protocols early in the year to help students get into the habit of using specific observations. Both are used for works in progress, though Getting Suggestions is better done early in a work in progress, and What Do You See is better near the end.

Details

The Getting Suggestions Protocol takes 15–20 minutes per round, while the whole What Do You See Protocol can be completed in 15–20 minutes.

The facilitator makes the scripts available in paper copies or a computer projection. The version below of What Do You See is designed for use with small works that can be passed from hand to hand. However, it can be easily adapted for use with larger works that require a gallery walk.

Steps

Getting Suggestions Protocol

1. Student 1 exhibits his or her artwork in progress, along with these two sentences ("scripts") completed in his or her sketchbook: "I feel that the most successful aspect of my work is _____." And "It would be helpful to hear your observations about _____."

2. Meanwhile, Students 2, 3, and 4 silently read the sentences in the sketchbook, and examine the work. Following this, they complete the following sentences in Student 1's sketchbook: "You asked for feedback about _____. What I especially notice is _____. I can imagine your doing _____ next because _____."

3. Student 1 reads all the peer comments in the sketchbook, then responds as follows: "As I understand your response to my work, you suggested _____, _____, and _____. I think I will try _____ because _____."

4. The process repeats until all the students have presented.

What Do You See Protocol

1. Each of four student artists working as a group around a table writes in his or her sketchbook: "I want to communicate _____ in my work. I think that I have done this by including _____."

2. Each artist then passes his or her small artwork to the right but holds on to his or her sketchbook. Each person has 1 minute to look at the work he or she receives, then write on a Post-it note: "This work makes me think _____ because I see _____ in it." Then the peer reviewer sticks the Post-it onto the work and passes it to the right.

3. The process repeats twice, but the reviewers are urged to respond independently without consideration to others' Post-its. Without looking at anyone else's comments, they stick the Post-it on the back

of the work. The work goes around the circle and comes back to the artist.

4. When all the artists have their own works back in hand, they read all the Post-its now affixed. Then in their sketchbooks they complete the following: "My peer artists saw _____, _____, and _____ in my work. The most generative of these responses for me at this point in my work is _____, and I plan to follow up by _____."

Facilitation Tips

The facilitator should bear in mind that the "scripts" are not mindless constraints, but challenges in themselves, and should clarify this point up front. For example, the scripts challenge the artists to reflect on their intentions, to exercise their perceptions, and to consider ways in which another's perceptions might prove generative for their own further work. Having students end by discussing how they felt about the feedback can hasten their growth as artists and connoisseurs.

Variations

Designed for the visual arts, these protocols can easily lend themselves to peer review of any artistic work and are particularly adaptable to online use.

Rich Text Protocol

This is a demanding protocol that Joe and Beth McDonald developed to help groups read and understand texts that need close reading and that yield greater understanding when approached element by element and layer by layer. The text that stimulated the development is an intriguing segment of a longer videotape that Ilene Kantrov and her colleagues developed at the Education Development Center (undated), and that she kindly allowed the McDonalds to use in their own teaching. The particular segment features a group of five upper-elementary-school students working together on a complicated math problem. Among the students is a boy with a red hat. We make reference to this video and to this boy in the steps listed below.

At the heart of the protocol is a theory of reading derived from the work of Robert Scholes (1985). It suggests the usefulness of bumps in the text—points of interest or puzzlement that can cause a reader to interrupt a smooth reading process and delve below the surface to explore his or her assumptions more critically. So the protocol begins with *noticing* points of interest or puzzlement, next exploring these in an *interpretive* phase, then ending with a *critical* phase in which participants share in writing a particular perspective they choose to apply to the text.

In format, this protocol (like several others) owes much to the Collaborative Assessment Conference described at the start of this chapter.

Purpose

This protocol is useful for dealing with a text that is dense or ambiguous in meaning or complicated in structure. It enables a group to "unpack" the text (written, video, or still visual)—that is, take it apart slowly, element by element and layer by layer. Of course, one does the same thing in an ordinary text-based discussion without benefit of a protocol, but the protocol makes the analysis more transparent. Thus it serves as a good scaffold for learning text-based discussion habits.

Details

The protocol is designed for use by groups of 5 to 15 participants. It can run in variable amounts of time, depending on the length or format of the text, but generally takes about 1 hour. The facilitator provides the text and must be deeply familiar with it, having read or watched it several times. It is best to use short, demanding texts in any medium. We have used variations of the protocol in exploring a poem about a child's silence in class, a photograph of students taking a standardized test, a brief but rich account of three different students' attempts to understand a complex concept in economics, and the 7-minute portion of video featuring a boy wearing a red hat.

Chart paper or another medium for recording comments and keeping track of the layers of discussion is essential.

Steps

1. *Introduction.* The facilitator briefly describes the content of the text the group is about to "read," and previews the steps involved in the reading.
2. *Reading and noticing.* The facilitator provides sufficient time for participants to experience the text—for example, reading their own copy of a print text or viewing a video together. Participants are asked to notice elements of the text that interest, puzzle, or surprise them, jotting these down as they read, watch, or listen.
3. *Sharing.* In a go-round each participant shares one to three elements they noticed—for example, "The boy with the red hat never

spoke" or "The poet starts off using some punctuation and drops it completely by the third stanza." Although it is often difficult to separate noticing from interpreting, the facilitator tries to discourage the latter. "A noticing," he or she may say, "is something that we can check the validity of just by checking the text. We don't need any outside information or expertise." The facilitator does not permit participants to comment on one another's offerings at this point. The facilitator records all the noticings on chart paper.

4. *Checking*. In this step the facilitator asks the group if there is anything on the list from Step 3 that needs "checking out" before moving on. For example, a participant may say, "I didn't notice that the boy with the red hat never spoke. Can we check that out?" When the text is a written one, it is easy to do the checking as each request is made. However, for videotapes, it is best to get the whole list of requests out first and then check them all out during a second viewing. The facilitator may again have to caution the group to keep the focus on noticing rather than on interpreting. Did the boy in the red hat speak or not? At this point, commentary about why the boy did or did not speak is not permitted. As noticings are checked, the facilitator circles them on the chart paper or puts a check mark by them.

5. *Interpreting*. During this step, the facilitator guides the group in the selection of two or three items from the chart paper that would be fruitful or interesting to interpret further. This is a judgment call based on the size of the group and the time available. The facilitator leads a go-round for each point selected. For example, during the round someone may say that the boy in the red hat does not speak because he is intimidated by the rest of the group. Someone else may suggest that he feels incompetent with respect to the problem and cannot find an entry point. No direct challenges to the interpretations are permitted, but the facilitator encourages alternative interpretations of the same phenomenon. The various interpretations of each element are duly noted on chart paper.

6. *Identifying a perspective*. In this step the facilitator asks participants to select one idea from the text under study and to write about it, based on a particular perspective or theory that they bring to it. The facilitator should define this theory or perspective as "some overarching idea—for example, about teaching and learning—that you might bring to any text you read about teaching and learning, or that seems particularly relevant to this text." For example, one participant may write that the speechlessness of the boy with the red hat provides vivid evidence of how a child who is shy or learning-disabled may become lost in a classroom where too much emphasis is put on small-group

discussion. Another may write that the boy with the red hat exhibits the characteristics of an English language learner and may well be learning more than he appears to be.

7. *Pair-share*. Participants pair off and share their writing with each other, challenging each other as appropriate.

8. *Final go-round*. One at a time, participants say one thing about the whole text, based on their experience with the protocol.

9. *Reflection*. The facilitator invites volunteers to comment on this reading experience.

Facilitation Tips

The facilitator should feel free to model each step by offering an example of the kind of response called for. He or she should also feel free to trim a noticing or an interpretation as needed. For example, someone might say in Step 2: "One of the girls seems to be just doing the scribing. She is the group's secretary, but is not doing any math learning. Typical pattern for many girls in math." And the facilitator might respond, "At the level of just noticing, let's say at this point that the shorter girl does much of the group's writing but little of its math talking. Somebody can ask us to check that out in the next step if they want. And in still another step, somebody can offer an interpretation of what's going on here and why."

Variation

After completing Step 1, a large group (e.g., 12–15) might break into work groups of three or four each to complete subsequent steps, recording their results as they go. They might also attempt to create a joint perspective in Step 6. Then small groups could combine to share (and challenge) each other's perspectives, or each small group could read aloud its final result to the whole group, inviting questions and comments.

CHAPTER 6

Working Toward Equity

Many protocol pioneers, often gathering in what they called "critical friends groups," used protocols to address inequities in education (in students' experiences and learning outcomes, and in educators' relationships with each other). They borrowed the term *critical friends group* from a 1993 article in *Educational Leadership* by Art Costa and Bena Kallick. In this influential article, the authors call for the widespread use in educational settings of a process for professional growth and school improvement that combines questioning, critique, careful listening; a willingness to try on new lenses; and an overall spirit of advocacy by colleagues for other colleagues and their work. Trust is a crucial lubricant for this process, as Costa and Kallick point out, though trust may be hard to find in situations where inequity is rife. Paradoxically, however, trust is also a consequence of the critical friends process. Thus these protocol pioneers bravely engaged in what must have seemed counterintuitive work: opening themselves and their practices to collegial scrutiny even where trust was scarce at first. But they did so in order to illuminate inequity, help dissipate it, and in the process produce sufficient trust to keep going. In the end, they hoped to ensure benefits for vulnerable students and their communities. In this regard, the pioneers targeted racial inequity in particular. In navigating what often proved to be the challenging terrain of local race relations, they trusted in well-facilitated protocols to provide the safety necessary for frank talk, thoughtful listening, and difficult learning. In the process, many of the groups they worked with discovered an opportunity gap below the surface of a predictable student achievement gap by race.

In this chapter, we borrow from the work of these pioneers. We also call attention to the need for continued creativity and boldness in this area. At the same time, we are mindful of the sensitivity of such work and the necessarily developmental nature of it. In general, we advocate jumping in when it comes to learning to use protocols, though *not* in this area. Jumping in too quickly or too intensely here can polarize and paralyze groups. That is why our chapter on equity is next to the last one: not because the topic is less important than others—hardly—but because people have to be ready to tackle it. On the other hand, it is also possible to be too cautious in this area. We all have to guard against what our friend Victor Cary, Senior Director of the National Equity Project, suggests is the tendency to think of inequity—racial inequity in particular—as undiscussable. It seems undiscussable, he explains, because of its roots in conditions of oppression which those not oppressed may have a hard time seeing or facing. The consequence is that real and daily encounters with inequity (which happen also to be rich learning opportunities) are often pushed underground into merely implicit awareness, coded speech, fear, guilt, and resentment. Structured protocols, Cary adds, can be crucial in bringing them up from this underground.

But how are we to manage the dilemma of *facing up* to the need to work toward equity without *jumping in* awkwardly? We have three suggestions:

1. Stay alert for good opportunities and grab them when they come. Good opportunities to engage issues of equity are most likely to arise where facilitators actively seek them, and where colleagues have learned in general to ask questions that make invisible things visible and unspeakable things discussable.

2. As you hone your protocol facilitation skills with other foci, pay attention to how the protocols might be tweaked to include an equity lens. As we illustrate below, this may be as simple as adding a single question.

3. Become acquainted with the protocols in this chapter, so you'll be ready when an opportunity arises to use one of them.

The first three protocols included here explore the diversity present in every human group, and aim to help participants see it and attend to it. They are Diversity Rounds, the Constructivist Listening Dyad, and the Cosmopolitan Protocol. Although they implicitly acknowledge diversity's insistent companion—namely, inequity—they do so gently. This is one reason why they make good starting points for protocol-based work on equity. All of them set the stage for deeper work. The protocol that follows these, the Looking at Data Protocol, might well have been featured in Chapter 5—about exploring texts—since it is an all-around good protocol for exploring data sets. We put it here, however—as the first of a set of four protocols that explicitly focus on inequity—for two reasons. The first is to illustrate how one can appropriate many different kinds of protocols in pursuit of an equity purpose—just as one can in looking at student work, or working on problems of practice; and the second is to emphasize the historic use of data in uncovering and addressing inequity. The last three protocols in the chapter also focus, as we suggest, on inequity. The Paseo illuminates the enormous diversity of a midsize to large group of people, then literally makes them stop to look at and speak about the inequity that attends this diversity. And both the Equity Protocol and the protocol called Looking at Student Work (with Equity in Mind) take the search for inequity and the effort to redress it into teaching—though with different slants.

Diversity Rounds

Nancy Mohr and Judith Scott had been working with a group of secondary school teachers in Indiana, exploring the principles of the Coalition of Essential Schools. Having worked with this same group for quite some time, they realized that it was time to challenge the group a bit, especially around issues related to diversity and equity. They developed this activity as a means of stimulating a conversation.

In each round, members of the group subdivided according to a particular "identifier" called out by Mohr or Scott: first the subject they taught, then where they grew up, and next their gender. During each round, members of the subgroups discussed the impact on their professional lives of the particular identifier. Nancy noted that the men stood around perplexed and fairly silent when it came time to discuss the impact of their gender on their professional lives. Not so the women.

Then, in the final round, the group of 80 teachers regrouped by "race." There was a gasp as the 79 White teachers went to one side of the room and the lone Black teacher to the other. In the process of debriefing the activity, the White people said how much fun the early rounds had been and how uncomfortable the last—one person suggesting that it must have been *very* uncomfortable for the sole Black teacher. The Black teacher, however, expressed her appreciation. The discomfort for her had surfaced long before the final round, when she recognized that apart from one of the cofacilitators, she was the only Black person present. Acknowledging this fact actually helped. "I was *well* aware that I was the only Black person in the room," she told her colleagues. "Now you too are well aware."

Purpose

One purpose of this protocol is to help participants become more aware of the various differences that exist among members of a human community and also the connections these members have to others. Another purpose is to help participants understand the impact of personal identity on professional experience. The activity is most useful for groups of participants who will be working together over an extended time.

Details

Especially effective with large groups, Diversity Rounds can be under-taken with almost any group of more than 20 members. The space must allow for people to move around. The rounds are best done standing the entire time.

Steps

1. *Introduction.* The facilitator explains that the participants will be asked to group and then regroup themselves three to five times, according to certain identity criteria, and that they will be moving about as they do this. The facilitator explains that the identities are purposefully vague and that participants will have to define them in their own way. Once in a particular grouping, participants will be prompted to talk about how the group's identity has shaped them as professionals.

2. *Grouping.* The facilitator asks participants to find people who are from the same group as they—for example, "Find people who come from the same place as you do." Typically people need encouragement to get moving. After they have formed groups, the facilitator reminds them to introduce themselves to each other and talk about how "coming from that area" has had an impact on them as professionals. (5–10 minutes, depending on the size of the group)

3. *Reporting.* The facilitator gives a 1-minute warning, then asks groups to report out a little of what they discussed. (5 minutes)

4. *Regrouping.* After each group reports, the facilitator asks people to regroup by another category, and repeat the steps—for example, "Now regroup by place in your family." Other possible groupings: kind of high school you attended, decade of your birth, gender, race, family size, many others.

5. *Debriefing.* The facilitator asks participants how they felt during the activity and also how their feelings may have changed from one grouping to the next. He or she also asks them what they have learned about diversity and about how diversity affects professional experience.

Facilitation Tips

Getting participants to move for the first round is the most difficult. The facilitator should push hard for this. Past that, everyone begins to have fun. The laughter that develops as groups form and re-form signifies identity. One way to help participants appreciate the connection between identity and diversity—which Beverly Daniel Tatum (1992, 1999) explores well—is to press them to notice this laughter and to theorize about its causes.

It is helpful to use the same prompt for each round. For example, "How has where you grew up affected you as an educator? How has your ethnicity affected you as an educator?" Sticking with the same prompt helps to surface and make discussable the differentially felt impact of life factors. For example, many White people hardly perceive the impact of Whiteness on their lives, while most Black people readily perceive the impact of Blackness on theirs. The same thing might be said about people on either side of the distinction between straight and gay, or ability and disability.

It is important to do several rounds of what are likely unthreatening categories of difference before attempting an "uncomfortable" one—that is, where there is plainly a history of discrimination and possibly of personal hurt—for example, race, gender, ethnic identity, disability, or age. It is important also to be sensitive in debriefing a round that does face up to discomfort.

The prompts for regrouping need not be unambiguous. For example, a prompt mentioned above having to do with place in the family might puzzle people initially. Is it about birth order? But what about people who have no siblings, or were foster children or stepchildren, or who were adopted? Sensing such puzzlement and finding a way through it can be a powerful outcome of this protocol. The facilitator should discourage "correct answers" to the questions raised. "Birth order groupings work," he or she might say, "but other kinds of groupings work too. It depends on the diversity of the group."

Like all protocols, this one needs a purpose, and the purpose needs to be kept in mind. Is it just about helping the group appreciate the fact that it is, like most other groups, diverse in important ways? If so, three rounds are probably enough. Or are there particular issues related to diversity that the group needs to explore—for example, confronting and dealing with inequity? If so, more rounds may be needed. The facilitator should work at the edge of the group's comfort zone with regard to the basis of the groupings, but also be prepared to change plans depending on how things go.

Constructivist Listening Dyad

This simple but assertive protocol offers good preparation for working on equity. It presses for self-reflection, as Victor Cary of the National Equity Project suggests, even as it provides crucial practice in listening to others. Based on the work of Julian Weissglass (1990, 2002), the protocol works well in a range of contexts—including those that are intellectually and emotionally challenging. It makes a useful habitual practice too—that is, a customary activity of, say, a professional learning community. Indeed, in the hands of a skillful facilitator it is highly adaptable to a wide range of uses, including fostering equity. In this respect it goes a step beyond Diversity Rounds. In the face of diversity it implicitly invites people to engage in connection, and it teaches them how to do this safely and effectively.

Purpose

The purpose of this protocol is to help participants become better at talking in depth with others—and better at listening attentively in the process. On the surface it seems only to press for a respectful encounter. However, its deeper goal—achieved by practicing the protocol over time—is to foster tolerance for and delight in human difference.

Details

As its name suggests, the Constructivist Listening Dyad is for two participants, though their dyad typically convenes in a room full of other dyads. The key contract between the two dyad members is to *listen* to each other. To emphasize this point, Victor Cary stresses that the listeners need not make sense of what their partners are talking about. That is, they may lack the requisite conceptual or appreciative framework or cultural background for understanding it, or may misunderstand a crucial point. But still they listen assiduously. They give full attention and trust listening to bring them closer to understanding. This unusual contract frees the listeners—as well as the talkers—of the social expectation to "make sense," and of the self-imposed urgency to do so on what may be in many cases too fast a timeline. In contrast to other protocols that press for understanding, this one cuts some slack for the time often required to reach understanding.

The guidelines for Constructivist Listening are as follows:

- Each person is given equal time to talk about whatever he or she chooses to talk about—except that the talker may not criticize or complain about the listener or about mutual colleagues.
- The listener must listen intently, but may not break in with his or her own perspective, nor interpret, paraphrase, analyze, or give advice afterward.
- What is said and heard stays completely confidential.

Steps

1. *Setting the focus.* The facilitator begins by explaining that the purpose of the listening in a Constructivist Listening Dyad is to benefit the talker, and that the power of the process depends on the partners giving due attention to this purpose. To help participants grasp the point, the facilitator may engage them in some preliminary

discussion based on prompts like, "Think of a time when you felt really listened to. How did it feel? What was its value to you?" The facilitator might usefully prompt some conversation about qualities of good listening too—for example, "What does it look like? How exactly does a good listener listen? What happens in your mind while actively listening?" Following this discussion, the facilitator cites the guidelines given above and asks if anyone has clarifying questions concerning them.

2. *Setting the time.* Next, the facilitator sets the duration of the listening—from 2 minutes, equally split, for a practice round, to 4–10 minutes, equally split, for a regular round among experienced users or dyads. The facilitator must be conscientious in keeping the time, insisting on a strict apportionment of listening per dyad member, and signaling the shift with a timer or a small hand bell that he or she demonstrates in this step.

3. *Dyads proceed.* Dyads talk and listen according to the guidelines.

4. *Reflection.* The facilitator leads a general discussion of the process. Prompts might include: What came up for you? How did you feel as listener? How did you feel as talker? What benefit did you gain as talker? What was difficult for you? What came up for you reflecting on the prompt? What purpose might this protocol serve?

Facilitation Tip

Note that the protocol, as laid out above, does not explicitly address equity issues—or any other issues. Yet in an actual context participants will need to construe a practical use for this tool in order to engage with it fully. Typically, therefore, the facilitator points out at the beginning that the protocol trains us for the kind of listening that helps us cross cultural borders, and asks participants to list some situations in which listening well and crossing cultural borders are required. In a workshop or series of workshops focused on equity, he or she might also say in Steps 1 and 4, "Let's think about the ways that this intensive listening process might help us work on equity."

Victor Cary suggests that Constructive Listening is a liberating structure that scaffolds individuals and groups toward a unified affective field that builds trust over time for what he calls "Discourse II conversations." These are sometimes called "courageous conversations" or "fierce conversations" (see, e.g., Glenn Singleton and Curtis Linton's 2006 book, *Courageous Conversations about Race*). By any name, these are conversations that focus explicitly on issues of equity and that push all participants into constructive discomfort.

Cosmopolitan Protocol

This is a text-based protocol developed by Joe McDonald based on the philosopher Kwame Anthony Appiah's (2006) book, *Cosmopolitanism: Ethics in a World of Strangers*. Appiah argues that all humans have an obligation to strive for intercultural understanding, though without compromising their own values. "Cosmopolitans," he explains, "suppose that all cultures have enough overlap in their vocabulary of values to begin a conversation. But they don't suppose . . . that we could all come to agreement if only we had the same vocabulary" (p. 57).

Joe developed the protocol for the benefit of participants in an NYU summer program for aspiring college students. The students from South Bronx high schools were spending 4 weeks getting used to a college setting in Greenwich Village. They were not only reading and discussing Appiah's book (and in a relatively strange setting for them), but they were also eating "strange" food daily for lunch—falafel, sushi, dosas. And they were communicating online daily with other students in India, South Africa, England, and other places—part of a related project called Kidnet, in which youth from around the world share digital compositions (Hull, Stornaiuolo, & Sahni, 2010).

Those who use the protocol in other settings should think about how they might replicate these contextual advantages in their settings too. Are people at hand from different racial, ethnic, religious, or socioeconomic groups? Or might they be linked in via social networking? Are there some "strange" experiences participants might have together, comparable to eating sushi for the first time? Again, might the Internet help? Can everyone read and discuss some text prior to the protocol that explains the benefits of receiving each other's differences with open minds—that is, the benefits of cosmopolitanism. It might be Appiah's book, but it could also be something shorter and less challenging (particularly for younger readers).

Purpose

The purpose of this protocol is to explore "strange" cultural material without rushing to judgment; to try to see unfamiliar cultures, religions, societies, and so on from the perspective of people used to them; to postpone disagreement in order to gain greater understanding first. Not to set too grand an expectation, the purpose of this protocol is to gain more adherents to a tradition of living tolerantly with others that has been practiced at certain times and places throughout all of recorded human history, but that has also persistently and tragically been put aside at other times—and even in the same places.

Steps

1. *Introduction.* The facilitator introduces the protocol as an exercise in thinking—one that requires putting one's own values to the side for some moments in order to explore someone else's different values, perhaps "strange" values. "The purpose, however," the facilitator explains, "is not to agree with these different values, but rather simply to understand them."

2. *Introducing a text.* The facilitator introduces a reading, image, video, or other text that the participants read or view together, one that represents aspects of a culture with different values from those most participants already know. The values may be familial (e.g., regarding marriage or child-rearing), religious, political, sexual, and so on.

3. *Clarifying questions.* The facilitator prompts: "What do you need to ask in order to understand this other culture better?" The point is not necessarily to answer such questions, though if other participants have answers, they are encouraged to share them. In an online or blended version of the protocol, time might be set aside to answer such questions through web searches and sharing answers found. In any case, a fundamental purpose of the clarifying questions is to explore the strangeness rather than mitigate it.

4. *Believing in.* In this step, the facilitator asks participants to employ the first half of a thinking strategy that Peter Elbow (1986) calls methodological believing and doubting. They "believe in" some facet of the strange culture—for example, that under some circumstances a nation might reasonably ban a certain form of religious expression, that some groups might reasonably set themselves apart from other groups by starkly different dress or other behavior, that some benefits might derive from the practice of parents choosing their children's spouses, and so on. This "believing in" is not necessarily genuine; it is merely a way to "get inside" the other culture in order to get used to it, to begin to understand it better. Participants are asked—either in a go-round or by volunteering—to share a comment that derives from this effort to "believe in." The facilitator may encourage participation by asking participants to begin each comment with the phrase, "If I believed in this practice or [other manifestation of this 'strange' culture], I would . . . "

5. *Expressing doubt about.* The facilitator next asks participants to go the other way—to express doubt about some facet of this strange culture. Again, the doubting is not necessarily genuine.

6. *Open discussion.* In an open discussion, participants reflect on what

they have gained by way of understanding through the exercise of their believing and doubting "muscles."

The Paseo or Circles of Identity

The Paseo was developed by facilitators at the 2001 Winter Meeting of the National School Reform Faculty. The facilitators were putting the final touches on their agenda for what was to be a 2-day workshop for educators engaged with their critical friends groups. What became clear to the team of more than 20 facilitators, however, was that the agenda did not adequately address issues of equity generally, and racial equity in particular. The team felt the need for a protocol that might allow participants to enter this space quickly, deeply, and safely. After a fairly lengthy discussion and the development of some guiding principles, Debbi Laidley, with Debbie Bambino, Debbie McIntyre, Stevi Quate, and Juli Quinn, created the following protocol that was used by all groups at the beginning of the gathering. It is named for the evening stroll common in Spanish-speaking countries and neighborhoods. The implication of the name is that the protocol begins with a simple coming together, but can lead to deeper connections.

Purpose

The Paseo is a tool for initiating dialogue when a group would like to talk about issues of identity, diversity, beliefs, and values—and the role that these play in educational work.

Details

The protocol begins with silent reflection by the participants but moves on to an activity that requires open space, and ends with a large-group discussion.

Steps

1. *Mapping identity.* Each participant draws a web with his or her name at the center, and identity descriptors linked to it. For example, one participant might write "Arthur," and then "Black," "grew up in Alabama," "gay," "teacher," and so on. The facilitator prompts the participants to include descriptors that have especially shaped them as people and affected their interactions with the world. They then carry this drawing through the next two steps.

2. *Preparing for the paseo.* The entire group then moves to stand in a large open area, forming two concentric circles. An even number of people is necessary, since the dialogue takes place in pairs. For uneven groups, a volunteer can play roving observer, and use his or her observations to begin the final step.

3. *Dialogue in paseo.* The facilitator next begins a series of prompts that will lead to one-on-one dialogue between members of the concentric circles based on their web drawings. Members of the outer circle rotate clockwise between questions. The facilitator allows for a brief wait time before each dialogue begins. Appropriate prompts include the following:

   - With which two descriptors on your web do you identify most strongly and why?
   - With which descriptors do you believe others identify you most strongly, and how do you feel about this?
   - Talk briefly about a time when one of the elements of your identity worked to your advantage.
   - Talk briefly about a time when one of the elements of your identity worked to your disadvantage.
   - Talk briefly about a time when you noticed an inequity (involving you or others) but did not acknowledge it openly.
   - Talk about a time when you noticed an inequity (involving you or others) and said or did something to address it.

4. *Debriefing.* In the case where there is an observer (the "odd" participant), the facilitator asks him or her to begin the debriefing with observations in response to the general prompt: "What have we gained from this dialogue in paseo about equity and inequity?" The facilitator then follows up by calling on others to comment.

Facilitation Tips

True to its metaphorical roots, the paseo should move slowly—with time for participants to think as well as talk. The facilitator should stay aware of the emotional and physical energy level of the group—in terms of how many questions to ask, and how long to sustain each round. Some mobility-challenged participants may need a chair stationed in the circle that does not rotate.

Some facilitators may choose to allow pairs to stay together for the last two questions because of the complementary nature of the questions, or to manage the rotation (e.g., inside circle moves two people on the next step) so that everyone ends up back with his or her starting partner.

Looking at Data Protocol

This is one of two complementary data-focused protocols in this new edition of the book. The other is in Chapter 4, and is called What Do We Know? What Do We Suspect? What Do We Need to Find Out? As that title may suggest, it deals with the broad process of inquiry relative to some focus—a focus that might well be equity. The protocol here, by contrast, guides the analysis of a single data set, and in this chapter we suggest a data set relevant to equity.

The Looking at Data Protocol was initially designed by Joe McDonald for a network of New York City charter schools (the PICCS Network at the Center for Educational Innovation—Public Education Association). Marlene Roy and Terra Lynch, in their Facilitative Leadership Seminar at the NYU Metro Learning Communities, later adapted the protocol for use by other schools. The protocol is inspired in part by the work of Kathryn Boudett, Elizabeth City, and Richard Murnane (2013), as captured in their book *Data Wise*; and by Dan Koretz's (2008) book *Measuring Up: What Educational Testing Really Tells Us*. Anyone using protocols for data analysis should read these valuable books.

At its heart, the Looking at Data Protocol is a simple text-based protocol where the text is a single data set. Like other text-based protocols, it encourages close attention to details, and low inference at first. The data set we imagine here for illustrative purposes portrays school-level results from a recent state assessment in reading, disaggregated by grade level, race, gender, income level (measured by free and reduced lunch status), and ability/disability status (measured by the existence or not of an Individualized Educational Plan or IEP). This is, of course, exactly the kind of data set that an equity-minded school faculty would be eager to explore, and one that is either readily available, or easy to assemble.

Purpose

The general purpose of this protocol is to gain collective insight from a data set. The specific purpose, as we construe it for the purposes of this chapter, is to focus this pursuit of insight on equity and inequity.

Details

The protocol can be completed in 1 hour or less, depending on the number of participants (4 to 10 or more), and the times allotted to each step. It is best used by a group of participants who have developed norms of collegiality associated with a professional learning community. These typically include a sense of common purpose and joint responsibility, a willingness to ban blame and defensiveness, openness to speculation, and generosity toward others' perceptions even when they may differ from one's own. If the participants do not already share these norms, it is important to begin the meeting with a brief listing of them and a request for consensus in maintaining them.

In the version we present below, one participant serves as presenter (which involves a little preparation as in Step 1), another as facilitator, and a third as recorder.

Steps

1. *Planning.* The presenter familiarizes himself or herself with the data set in preparation for Step 2. This may in some circumstances require expert support—for example, from the school's data coach.
2. *Orientation.* The presenter offers an orientation to the data set. This may include, for example, what the columns, rows, and cells contain, what abbreviations mean, how best to read the tables, and so on. He or she asks participants to hold questions for Step 3. (3 minutes)
3. *Focus question.* The presenter suggests a focus question for the group's reading of the data. This is likely one that is related to a priority that the group or school has set—for example: "What do the data here suggest about opportunity to learn in our school based on race?"or "How are our lower income readers doing in comparison to our higher-income readers across grade levels and other demographic factors?" Note that the question need not be one that can be entirely answered with numerical data alone, and thus the protocol may feed a larger inquiry, including efforts to find out more. (3 minutes)
4. *Clarifying questions.* Participants ask questions on matters that they find unclear or confusing, and that they think the presenter may be able to clarify. If the presenter cannot easily answer, and if collective pondering yields little, then the questions are deferred for later expert consultation. (5 minutes)
5. *Flagging.* Participants work in teams of two or three to call attention to particular data within the data set that may prove especially relevant to the focus question. They do not necessarily need to explain—or even fully understand themselves—why they think attention is warranted. A hunch about relevance is good enough. The recorder notes the flagged data—for example, by highlighting cells. Discussion is not permitted at this point. (10 minutes)
6. *Making inferences.* Participants work in teams of two or three to make inferences based on particular elements of the data set, whether or

not these elements have been flagged in the previous step. The facilitator encourages low-level inferences related to the focus question, but does not rule out inferences that may seem beyond the focus. Sometimes, what seem out-of-focus remarks prove valuable in the next steps. Again, no discussion about or questioning of inferences is permitted in this step. The goal is brainstorming. The recorder records all the inferences on poster paper or by computer projection. (10 minutes)

7. *Discussion.* The facilitator invites open discussion about both the data elements that surfaced in Step 4 and the inferences that surfaced in Step 5. The recorder continues to record. (10 minutes or more)
8. *Stepping back.* In a go-round, participants state briefly what they see as next steps for the group, given their analysis and discussion. These may include additional clarification, further inquiry, or action. (5 to 10 minutes)

Equity Protocol

Like the Paseo above, the Equity Protocol originated at the December 2001 Winter Meeting of the National School Reform Faculty in Houston. It is a kind of screening tool used by colleagues to help each other detect possible inequity in their own teaching.

Details

A teacher-presenter brings an assignment and corresponding student work on which he or she would like feedback using an equity lens. The student work is typically a whole class set. The facilitator and the teacher meet beforehand and agree to a set of equity-focused questions that seem appropriate. Optimal group size is 9 to 12—among which 3 or 4 duplicate sets of student work can easily be shared.

Steps

1. *Presentation.* The teacher presents the assignment to the group, as well as the original expectations for resulting student work. The presenter also offers any context that may be appropriate—for example, the curriculum context; the grade level; the range of achievement levels of the class overall; and a break-down of the class by race, gender, poverty, ability/disability, and English language learners.
2. *Go-rounds on the assignment.* Following a silent reading of the assignment by the group, the facilitator leads several go-rounds, each focused on a question. Possible questions include the following:

- What do you see in the assignment that might be engaging to many different students?
- What do you see that might meet more than one learning modality?
- What do you see that might support/hinder students with special needs?
- What do you see that might support/hinder English language learners?
- What do you see that might be considered bias in the language used in the assignment?
- What do you wonder about with respect to the equity of this assignment?

3. *Student work.* The presenter silently distributes the student work sample. Meanwhile, the facilitator discusses the terms of engagement with the sample—typically, silent reading with skimming encouraged, notetaking relative to equity concerns (though not on the sample itself), and the sharing of packets. Participants are given sufficient time to review the work. (at least 15 minutes for a whole-class sample)

4. *Final go-round.* The facilitator asks each participant to reflect on the relationship between the questions raised earlier and the student work reviewed, citing in each case evidence from the reading. The facilitator cautions that the purpose of this round is not to make judgments, but to raise further questions. (5–10 minutes)

5. *Reflection.* The presenter reflects on all that he or she has heard, answers (undefensively) any questions that have arisen, and shares any new insights he or she may have gained. (5 minutes)

6. *Open conversation.* The facilitator engages all participants in an open conversation, using the following prompt: "What do we think we have learned from this experience about equity and efforts to achieve it?"

Facilitation Tip

One crucial challenge here, as in any protocol where teachers dare to share their own and their students' work, is to ensure that the teachers do not emerge from the experience feeling in some sense "blamed"—for an imperfect assignment, an inequitable arrangement, and so forth. It helps if the facilitator acknowledges that every assignment is imperfect, and that inequity frequently intrudes unseen. He or she might then "ban blame"—no blame assigned, no defenses raised—and declare that ownership of the work presented and the responsibility for its improvement will be collective. We associate the phrase "ban blame" with James Comer's School Development

Program—a 40-year pioneer of effective and equitable school reform—with its emphasis on no-fault problem solving (see medicine.yale.edu/childstudy/comer/index.aspx).

Looking at Student Work (with Equity in Mind)

Nancy Mohr modified many standard protocols to make sure that equity issues were front and center. Here is her equity-focused adaptation of the Collaborative Assessment Conference (see Chapter 5 for the original protocol). True to its source, and unlike the Equity Protocol above, the focus of this protocol is more on the student work (and the traces of inequity it may manifest) than on the assignment.

Purpose

The purpose of the protocol is to embed a focus on equity in the collaborative examination of student work and thus spur specific equity-minded action as a follow-up.

Details

The protocol requires roughly an hour. It may be undertaken in any group of 10–15 participants, but is best undertaken as a regular feature of a smaller professional learning community that meets regularly.

Steps

1. *Introductions.* The facilitator welcomes the presenter and other participants (who are ideally potential presenters themselves in a recurring activity), and raises the protocol's orienting question: "What possible traces of inequity of any kind and from any source do you see in this student work sample?" He or she also says that the purpose is to practice noticing inequity and to speculate about enrichment strategies that can address it. The purpose is *not*, he or she adds, to assess blame.

2. *Presentation.* The presenter has brought several samples of student work in response to the same assignment. Preferably, the overall set represents different levels of accomplishment and has been selected with equity in mind (e.g., mixed by race, gender, or ability/disability). The presenter also describes the assignment and identifies data relevant to the question—for example, the gender/racial identities of the students in the sample, and the gender/racial achievement data of the school and/or classroom as a whole.

3. *Quiet review.* Participants quietly examine the work sample with the question in mind.
4. *Description.* Participants say what they see in the sample that *may be* relevant to the focus question. The emphasis here is on spotting possibly relevant details without making more than low-level inferences. Here the presenter remains silent, and may not comment, even at the end of the step or to clarify the context.
5. *Student empathy.* Here the participants speculate on how one or more students in the sample seem to have *related* in any sense to the assignment—for example, in terms of interest, intellectual challenge, comfort level, drawing on previous knowledge, level of engagement, and so on. Again, the presenter remains silent.
6. *Speculations.* In this step, the participants speculate—based on their reading of the sample and their empathic efforts—on ways to enrich the learning opportunities of one or more students represented in the sample. For example, a participant might say, "I think student #3 would benefit from opportunities to read her writing aloud in a small peer group or with a single partner."
7. *Presenter responds.* Here the presenter responds to anything that he or she cares to respond to, reserving the opportunity to think more about other matters. The facilitator introduces this step by reminding all of the protocol norm to ban blame—which implicitly also bans defensiveness. "We do this," he or she might say, "because inequity is everywhere—including in all our work—and we're training ourselves to notice it."
8. *Open conversation.* The protocol ends with open conversation about the sample (assignment and student work) by the light of the focus question—with an opportunity for the presenter to have the final word.

Facilitation Tips

The tone set by the facilitator in this protocol is crucial to its success. It must be open and unanxious—as if a teacher welcoming colleagues to examine his or her work for evidence of inequity were simply the most ordinary of collegial activities and certainly not cause for apprehension. The trick is to welcome this experience as beneficial for all, to help the presenter be comfortable (in the protocol itself as well as before and after), and to insist cheerfully but also resolutely on the norm that bans blame (and defensiveness). As always, however, the facilitator should be prepared to redress any impropriety—for example, to quickly counteract a remark that violates the no-blame norm with a terse, "Remember, no blame or defensiveness allowed in this protocol."

CONCLUSION

Jumping In

In Chapter 1 we introduced a persistent theme of this book with the expression "educating ourselves." We put this expression in the form of the first-person plural to signify that we authors are educators too and, like all our fellow educators, in need of continual education. We meant the phrase also as a call to join with us and many other educators who struggle to educate ourselves within sometimes indifferent institutions, because we know our students' learning depends ultimately on our own.

Throughout the book, though, we have used third-person pronouns, especially in describing the work of the facilitator. We have wanted our readers to gain a comprehensive view of the role—from the one who conducts a simple go-round with some colleagues on a small task force, to the one who leads an institution's comprehensive effort to study itself and its impact on students, drawing partly on a slice. Knowing that we are likely to have a range of readers with a range of purposes in their reading, we know also that most are unlikely to find themselves facilitating all the protocols described in the book.

In closing, however, we want to invite all readers to facilitate at least some of them. So we come full circle with our pronouns. We encourage *you* to jump in. Remember our claim: that we can have the kinds of genuinely accountable institutions of learning that our students need only if many of us who work in educational institutions are willing to learn how to take the lead in educating ourselves. And if *you* have taken the trouble to read this book, then certainly *you* are likely to be or to become a facilitative leader.

How can you become such a leader, if you are not already one? The only way to learn this work is by doing it. Being transparent and open about what you are trying allows for jumping in, with opportunities to talk about the results afterward. And the courage you show enables participants to become engaged and helps build community.

WAYS TO GET STARTED

- Try these protocols in any environment. Why not a committee meeting, a leadership team, or a task force? Volunteer to facilitate.

- Get a partner to work with. Partnering is good for morale and for honing each other's skills.
- Seek opportunities to work on facilitation skills through workshops and classes.
- Form a group to support one another, what we call a "critical friends group." Meet regularly, and don't just make promises; keep them.
- Try these activities with students.
- Solicit someone to act as a coach—someone who will sit in while you work and give you feedback.
- Observe other facilitators.

THINGS THAT MAKE IT EASIER

- Not skipping norms. Norms can make it clear that you are trying something new and that it's okay if it isn't totally successful the first time around. Make sure one of the norms promotes risk-taking.
- Not skipping reflecting/debriefing afterward. If you don't do it, people may be less aware of what they've learned and thus less likely to build on it. And you may learn less than you otherwise might about facilitating well.
- Not being afraid of silence. Learn to listen. Worry less about what to say. Let the participants do the "saying."
- Being honest about the fact that you have some concerns yourself, while acknowledging that your hopes in the possibilities can overcome them.
- Remembering that this is like any sport, art form, or game: You learn by doing. If you try to understand all of the rules first, you'll never get started.
- Really believing that most of the wisdom to be gained will come from the participants.
- Not involving people simply for "buy-in," but because their voices are crucial to everybody's learning.
- Remembering that there are very few mistakes you can make that would be (as our computers sometimes warn) "fatal errors." Maybe mild embarrassment. Think of this as an opportunity to model vulnerability.
- Having the courage, above all, to do business differently, to be a learner, to be a leader, to educate yourself.

References

Allen, D. (Ed.). (1998). *Assessing student learning: From grading to understanding.* New York: Teachers College Press.

Allen, D., & Blythe, T. (2004). *The facilitator's book of questions: Tools for looking together at student and teacher work.* New York: Teachers College Press.

Appiah, K. A. (2006). *Cosmopolitanism: Ethics in a world of strangers.* New York: W. W. Norton.

Applebaum, E., Bailey, T., Berg, P., & Kalleberg, A. L. (2000). *Manufacturing advantage: Why high-performance work systems pay off.* Ithaca, NY: ILR Press.

Argyris, C., & Schön, D. A. (1996). *Organizational learning II: Theory, method, and practice.* Reading, MA: Addison-Wesley.

Aronson, E., & Patnoe, S. (1997). *The jigsaw classroom: Building cooperation in the classroom* (2nd ed.). New York: Longman.

Avidon, E. (2000). Context. In M. Himley (with P. Carini) (Eds.), *From another angle: Children's strengths and school standards* (pp. 24–26). New York: Teachers College Press.

Barrett, J., & Wasserman, N. (1987). *Risotto.* New York: Macmillan.

Blythe, T., Allen, D., & Powell, B. S. (2007). *Looking together at students' work* (2nd ed.). New York: Teachers College Press. (Original work published 1999)

Bolman, L. G., & Deal, T. E. (1997). *Reframing organizations: Artistry, choice, and leadership* (2nd ed.). San Francisco: Jossey Bass.

Boudett, K. P., City, E. A., Murnane, R. J. (2013). *Data wise: A step-by-step guide to using assessment results to improve teaching and learning* (revised and expanded ed.). Cambridge, MA: Harvard Education Press.

Brown, J. S., & Duguid, P. (2000). *The social life of information.* Boston: Harvard Business School Press.

Brown, J. S., & Gray, E. S. (1995, October 31). The people are the company: How to build your company around your people. *Fast Company.* Retrieved on January 13, 2013, from www.fastcompany.com/26238/people-are-company

Bryk, A. S., Sebring, P. B., Allensworth, E., Luppescu, S., & Easton, J. Q. (2010). *Organizing schools for improvement: Lessons from Chicago.* Chicago: University of Chicago Press.

City, E. A., Elmore, R. F., Fiarman, S. E., & Teitel, L. (2009). *Instructional rounds in education: A network approach to improving teaching and learning.* Cambridge, MA: Harvard Education Press.

Costa, A. L., & Kallick, B. (1993). Through the lens of a critical friend. *Educational Leadership, 51*(2), 49–51.

Curry, M. W. (2008). Critical friends groups: The possibilities and limitations embedded in teacher professional communities aimed at instructional improvement and school reform. *Teachers College Record, 110*(4), 733–774.

Donovan, M. S., Bransford, J. D., & Pellegrino, J. W. (Eds.). (2000). *How people learn: Bridging research and practice.* Washington, DC: National Academy Press.

Eagleton, T. (1983). *Literary theory.* Oxford, UK: Blackwell.

Education Development Center. (n.d.). *Faces of equity, tape one.* [VHD tape] Newton, MA: Author.

Elbow, P. (1986). *Embracing contraries: Explorations in learning and teaching.* New York: Oxford University Press.

Featherstone, H. (1998). Studying children: The Philadelphia teachers' learning cooperative. In D. Allen (Ed.), *Assessing student learning: From grading to understanding* (pp. 66–86). New York: Teachers College Press.

Fishman, C. (1996, April 30). Whole Foods is all teams. *Fast Company.* Retrieved on January 13, 2013 from www.fastcompany.com/26671/whole-foods-all-teams

Glickman, C. D. (1998). *Renewing America's schools: A guide to school-based action.* San Francisco: Jossey-Bass.

Goffman, E. (1974). *Frame analysis: An essay on the organization of experience.* Cambridge: Harvard University Press.

Gray, J. (1992). *Men are from Mars, women are from Venus: A practical guide for improving your communication and getting what you want in your relationships.* New York: HarperCollins.

Greene, M. (1988). *The dialectic of freedom.* New York: Teachers College Press.

Hall, G. E., & Hord, S. M. (1987). *Change in schools: Facilitating the process.* Albany: State University of New York Press.

Haller, J. (1978). *The blue strawberry cookbook: Cooking (brilliantly) without recipes.* Boston: Harvard Common Press.

Himley, M. (with Carini, P. F.). (2000). *From another angle: Children's strengths and school standards.* New York: Teachers College Press.

Hirsch, E. D. (1999). *The schools we need: Why we can't have them.* New York: Random House.

Holtzapple, E. (2001). *Standards in practice: Year one evaluation.* Cincinnati, OH: Cincinnati Public Schools.

Hull, G. A., Stornaiuolo, A., & Sahni, U. (2010). Cultural citizenship and cosmopolitan practice: Global youth communicate online. *English Education, 42*(4), 331–367.

Ichniowski, C., Levine, D. I., Olson, C., & Strauss, G. (Eds.). (2000). *The American workplace: Skills, compensation, and employee involvement.* New York: Cambridge University Press.

Kohn, A. (2000). *The schools our children deserve: Moving beyond traditional classrooms and tougher standards.* Boston: Mariner Books/Houghton Mifflin.

Koretz, D. (2008). *Measuring up: What educational testing really tells us.* Cambridge, MA: Harvard University Press.

Lakoff, G. (2002). *Moral politics: How liberals and conservatives think* (2nd ed.). Chicago: University of Chicago Press.

Lakoff, G. (2004). *Don't think of an elephant! Know your values and frame the debate.* White River Junction, VT: Chelsea Green.

Lampert, M. (1985). How do teachers manage to teach? Perspectives on problems of practice. *Harvard Educational Review, 55*(2), 178–194.

Lampert, M. (2001). *Teaching problems and the problems of teaching.* New Haven, CT: Yale University Press.

Little, J. W., Gearhart, M., Curry, M., & Kafka, J. (2003). Looking at student work for teacher learning, teacher community, and school reform. *Phi Delta Kappan, 83*(3), 185–192.

Louis, K. S., Kruse, S. D., & Marks, H. M. (1996). Schoolwide professional community. In F. M. Newmann & Associates (Eds.), *Authentic achievement: Restructuring schools for intellectual quality* (pp. 179–203). San Francisco: Jossey-Bass.

McDonald, J. P. (1992). *Teaching: Making sense of an uncertain craft.* New York: Teachers College Press.

McDonald, J. P. (2001). Students' work and teachers' learning. In A. Lieberman & L. Miller (Eds.), *Caught in the action: Professional development for teachers* (pp. 209–235). New York: Teachers College Press.

McDonald, J. P. (2002). Teachers studying student work: Why and how? *Phi Delta Kappan, 84*(2), 120–127.

McDonald, J. P., Mohr, N., Dichter, A., & McDonald, E. C. (2003). *The power of protocols: An educator's guide to better practice* (1st ed.). New York: Teachers College Press.

McDonald, J. P., Klein, E., & Riordan, M. (2009). *Going to scale with new school designs: Reinventing high school.* New York: Teachers College Press.

McDonald, J. P., Zydney, J. M., Dichter, A., & McDonald, E. C. (2012). *Going online with protocols: New tools for teaching and learning.* New York: Teachers College Press.

McIntosh, P. (1989, July/August). White privilege: Unpacking the invisible knapsack. *Peace and Freedom,* 10–12.

McLaughlin, M. W., & Talbert, J. E. (2001). *Professional communities and the work of high school teaching.* Chicago: University of Chicago Press.

McLaughlin, M. W., & Talbert, J. E. (2006). *Building school-based teacher learning communities.* New York: Teachers College Press.

National Research Council. (2000). *How people learn: Brain, mind, experience, and school* (Expanded ed.). Washington, DC: National Academy Press.

Newmann, F. M. & Associates. (1996). *Authentic achievement: Restructuring schools for intellectual quality.* San Francisco: Jossey-Bass.

Newmann, F. M., & Wehlage, G. G. (1995). *Successful school restructuring.* Madison, WI: Center on Organization and Restructuring of Schools, University of Wisconsin.

Oakes, J., & Lipton, M. (1999). *Teaching to change the world.* New York: McGraw-Hill.

Phillips, J. (2003). Powerful learning: Creating learning communities in urban school reform. *Journal of Curriculum and Supervision, 18*(3), 240–258.

Resnick, L. B. (1987). Learning in school and out. *Educational Researcher, 16*(9), 13–20.

Sato, M. (1992). Japan. In H. Leavitt (Ed.), *Issues and problems in teacher education: An international handbook* (pp. 155–168). Westwood, CT: Greenwood Press.

Scholes, R. (1985). *Textual power: Literary theory and the teaching of English.* New Haven, CT: Yale University Press.

Schön, D. A. (1983). *The reflective practitioner: How professionals think in action.* New York: Basic Books.

Schön, D. A., & McDonald, J. P. (1998). *Doing what you mean to do in school reform: Theory of action in the Annenberg Challenge.* Providence, RI: Annenberg Institute for School Reform, Brown University.

Schön, D. A., & Rein, M. (1994). *Frame reflection: Toward the resolution of intractable policy controversies.* New York: Basic Books.

Seidel, S. (1998). Wondering to be done: The Collaborative Assessment Conference. In D. Allen (Ed.), *Assessing student learning: From grading to understanding* (pp. 21–39). New York: Teachers College Press.

Singleton, G. E., & Linton, C. W. (2006). *Courageous conversations about race: A field guide for achieving equity in schools.* Thousand Oaks, CA: Corwin Press.

Stigler, J. W., & Hiebert, J. (1999). *The teaching gap: Best ideas from the world's teachers for improving education in the classroom.* New York: Simon & Schuster.

Supovitz, J. A. (2002). Developing communities of instructional practice. *Teachers College Record, 104*(8), 1591–1626.

Supovitz, J. A., & Christman, J. B. (2003). *Developing communities of instructional practice: Lessons from Cincinnati and Philadelphia.* Philadelphia, PA: Consortium for Policy Research in Education, University of Pennsylvania.

Talbert, J. E. (2011). Collaborative inquiry to expand student success in New York City schools. In J. A. O'Day, C. S. Bitter, & L. M. Gomez (Eds.), *Education reform in New York City: Ambitious change in the nation's most complex school system* (pp. 131–156). Cambridge, MA: Harvard Education Press.

Tatum, B. D. (1992). Talking about race, learning about racism: The application of racial identity development theory in the classroom. *Harvard Educational Review, 62,* 1–24.

Tatum, B. D. (1999). *Why are all the black kids sitting together in the cafeteria? And other conversations about race* (Rev. ed.). New York: Basic Books.

Thomas, D., & Brown, J. S. (2011). *A new culture of learning: Cultivating the imagination for a world of constant change.* Lexington, KY: Authors.

Vescio, V., Ross, D., & Adams, A. (2008). A review of research on the impact of professional learning communities on teaching practice and student learning. *Teaching and Teacher Education, 24,* 80–91.

Watanabe, T. (2002). Learning from Japanese lesson study. *Educational Leadership, 59*(6), 36–39.

Weissglass, J. (1990). Constructivist listening for empowerment and change. *The Educational Forum, 54*(4), 351–370.

Weissglass, J. (2002). Inequity in mathematics education: Questions for educators. *The Mathematics Educator, 12*(2), 34–39.

Wells, P. (2001). *The Paris cookbook.* New York: HarperCollins.

Wenger, E. (1998). *Communities of practice: Learning, meaning, and identity.* Cambridge, England: Cambridge University Press.

White, E. (2006). *Presentation in honor of Nancy Mohr.* Denver: Winter Meeting of the National School Reform Faculty.

Wilson, T. A. (1996). *Reaching for a better standard: English school inspection and the dilemma of accountability for American public schools.* New York: Teachers College Press.

Index

Protocols
  close textual analysis and, 5–7
  collaboration and, 8
  constraints of, 1–4
  democracy and, 8
  distributed leadership and, 8, 10
  informal conversations *versus*, 3, 5
  as interference, 3–4
  "just talking" *versus*, 3, 5
  nature and origins, 1
  online, x, 7, 21, 28, 40–47
  research on, 8–10
  self-education through, 4–5, 114–115
  seminal protocols, 1–3
  teacher learning communities and,
    9–10, 12–13, 97
  tips to ease use of, 115
  transparency with, 7–8
  ways to get started using, 114–115
Provocative Prompts, 23–25

Quate, Stevi, 106
Questions
  clarifying, 2, 30, 31, 33, 35, 37, 65,
    67, 105, 109
  in Collaborative Assessment
    Conference, 3, 77
  in Do What You Mean to Do, 65
  focusing, 2, 109
  in Marvin's Model, 26
  in Minnesota Slice/Slice Protocol,
    58–59
  in New Design Protocol, 67, 68
  in Peeling the Onion, 37
  in Peer Review Protocol (Online), 46
  probing, 2, 31, 36, 37, 67
  in Shadow Protocol, 62
  in Stuff and Vision Protocol, 42
  in What Comes Up, 50
Quinn, Juli, 106
Quotations
  in Mars/Venus Protocol, 87–88
  in Provocative Prompts, 23–25

Reaction, in Tuning Protocol, 29
Reading

  in Collaborative Assessment
    Conference, 77
  in Jigsaw Protocol, 83
  in Mars/Venus Protocol, 87
  in Minnesota Slice/Slice Protocol, 58
  in Panel Protocol, 85
  in Rich Text Protocol, 94
Reflection
  in Collaborative Assessment
    Conference, 77
  in Constructivist Listening Dyad, 103
  in The Consultancy, 32
  in Descriptive Consultancy, 33, 34
  in Equity Protocol, 111
  in Final Word Protocol, 80
  in Issaquah Coaching Protocol, 35,
    36
  in Mars/Venus Protocol, 88
  in Minnesota Slice/Slice Protocol, 58
  Reflection on a Word opener, 18–19
  in Stuff and Vision Protocol, 42
  in Success Analysis Protocol, 39
Regrouping, in Diversity Rounds, 100
Rein, Martin, 32
Repeat, in What Comes Up, 50
Reporting
  in Diversity Rounds, 100
  in Success Analysis Protocol, 39
Resnick, Lauren B., 12
Response
  in Collaborative Assessment
    Conference, 77
  in Descriptive Consultancy, 33–34
  in Issaquah Coaching Protocol, 36
  in Looking at Student Work (with
    Equity in Mind), 113
  in New Design Protocol, 68
  in Peeling the Onion, 37
  in Peer Review Protocol (Online), 46
  in School Visit Protocol, 71
  in Stuff and Vision Protocol, 42
  in Tuning Protocol, 29
  in What Comes Up, 50
Restructured schools, 8–9
Review, in Looking at Student Work
    (with Equity in Mind), 113

About the Authors

Joseph P. McDonald is a professor of Teaching and Learning at New York University's Steinhardt School of Culture, Education, and Human Development. His research interests include the policies and practices of school reform, the deep dynamics of teaching, and the creation of new settings for teacher education. He was the first Director of Research at the Annenberg Institute for School Reform at Brown University, where he also taught for many years, and was Senior Researcher at the Coalition of Essential Schools. He is the author or coauthor of nine books, including *Teaching: Making Sense of an Uncertain Craft, Going to Scale with New School Designs,* and *Going Online with Protocols.* McDonald was a high school teacher for 17 years, and principal of a small public high school. He lives in New York City and Wareham, Massachusetts, with Beth McDonald and their West Highland Terrier, Harry.

Nancy Mohr was an educational consultant and director of the New York Center of the National School Reform Faculty at New York University. She worked also with the Center for Reinventing Education at the University of Washington, and with other projects and groups of educators throughout the United States and Australia. She was the founding principal of University Heights High School in the Bronx, where she served for 10 years. The school was the first new school to open as a member of the Coalition of Essential Schools. Nancy authored or coauthored many articles and book chapters including "Small Schools Are Not Miniature Large Schools" in Bill Ayers's book *A Simple Justice.* She died in 2003.

Alan Dichter is a former New York City teacher, principal, director of leadership and new school development, and local instructional superintendent. He helped create and oversee New York's Executive Leadership Academy, a program designed to help leaders develop and incorporate facilitative leadership practices. He is author of a number of articles on leadership and professional development and has consulted widely on issues related to top urban school reform. He has also worked as a coach/facilitator for the New York City Leadership Academy and most recently as director of leadership development for Portland, Oregon, public schools. He is the coauthor of *Going Online with Protocols*. He now does independent consulting and lives with his wife, Vivian, and sons, Ben and Jacob, back in New York City.

Elizabeth C. McDonald is a master teacher in the Department of Teaching and Learning in the Steinhardt School of Culture, Education, and Human Development at New York University. She co-leads NYU's introductory course in teacher education, of which multiple sections each semester are co-taught in New York City schools by NYC teachers. She has been an elementary and middle school teacher of students with special needs, a professional development specialist for the Rhode Island State Department of Education, and for 9 years an elementary school principal. She is a coauthor of *Going Online with Protocols*. She lives in New York City and Wareham, Massachusetts, with Joe McDonald and their West Highland Terrier, Harry.